JOHN ELWAY
Armed and Dangerous

By Clay Latimer

ADDAX
PUBLISHING
GROUP

Dedication

To Loraine, and Ralph and Elaine

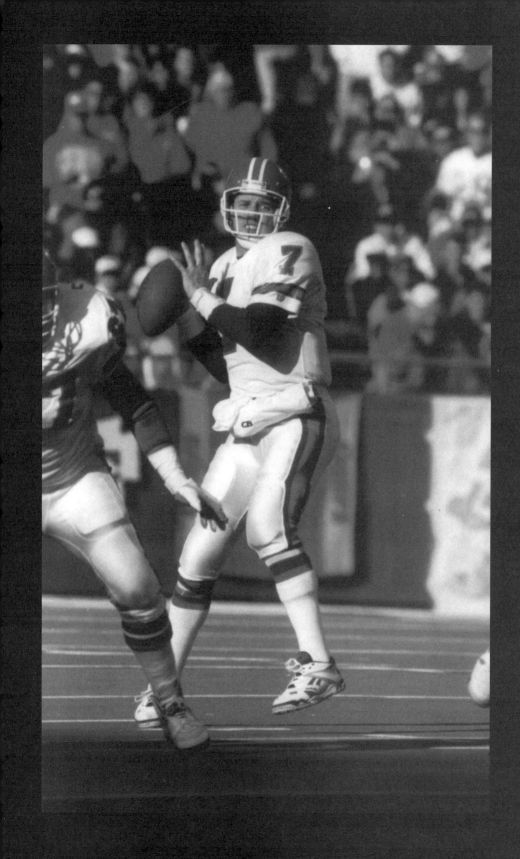

Table of Contents

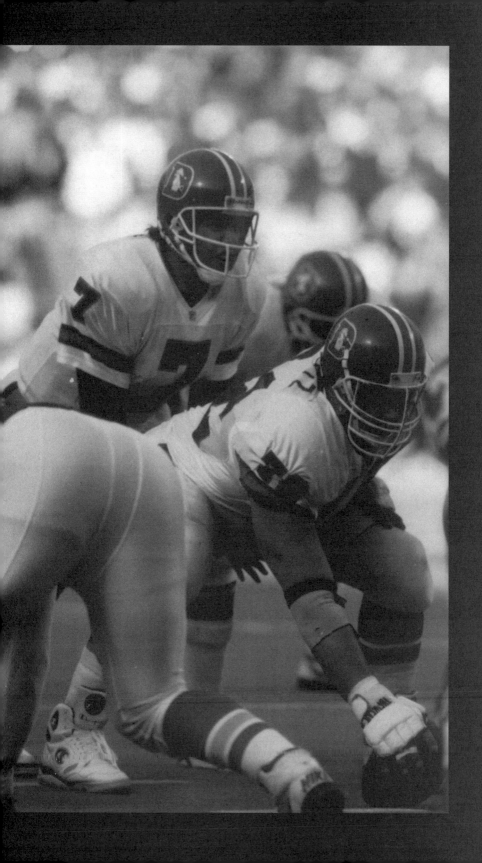

Acknowledgments

MOST BOOKS ARE COLLABORATIVE EFFORTS, AND THIS one is no exception.

The list of thanks should start with the *Rocky Mountain News* and *The Denver Post* and the beat work — over the years — of Rick Morrissey, Steve Caulk, T.J. Simers, Butch Brooks, Sam Adams, Adam Schefter, Jim Armstrong, Joseph Sanchez, John Henderson, Tom Kensler, Michael Knisley, and others. I'm also indebted to Bob Kravitz, Norm Clarke, Mark Wolf, Jay Mariotti, Woody Paige, Mark Kizla and Dick Connor. I trust I've kept their reporting and commentary in perspective.

I'd also like to thank my editors at the *Rocky Mountain News*, including Barry Forbis, who allowed me the freedom to complete this project, and Jim Saccomano, the Broncos' director of media relations, and his assistants, Paul Kirk and Richard Stewart.

I'd be remiss not to credit *Sports Illustrated, Sport, Football Digest, Beckett Football Monthly, Newsweek, The Bremerton Sun* and other publications too numerous to mention.

Thanks also to several illuminating books, including *The Quarterbacks* by Mickey Herskowitz, *The Pro Football Chronicle* by Dan Daly and Bob O'Donnell, *Great Ones* by Beau Riffenburgh and David Boss, *War Stories from the Field* by Joseph Hession and Kevin Lynch, *Super Bowl Chronicles* by Jerry Green, *John Elway* by Mark Stewart, *Orange Madness* by Woody Paige and *The Color Orange* by Russell Martin.

I'm especially indebted to Roland Lazenby as well as the people at Addax Publishing, including Darcie Kidson and Bob Snodgrass, whose patience and professional insights were invaluable.

My wife, Loraine, however, gets the first-place medal for patience.

Introduction

By Clay Latimer

BEFORE JOHN ELWAY ARRIVED IN 1983, IT TOOK A FIRM ACT of imagination for Denver Broncos fans to envision a Super Bowl on the Rocky Mountain horizon.

The team had finished the strike-shortened 1982 season with a 2-7 record, its first losing season since 1975. Three season-ending losses had left players weary and wary of the future, to say nothing of coach Dan Reeves.

But when Elway flew in for a whirlwind press conference, Broncos fans were blown away.

John Elway had raw star quality, he spoke in full paragraphs, he was school-boy earnest, he represented the promise of promise. And his arm was a fearsome weapon of mass production.

Not for a while, though.

Within months, Elway was sagging under the gathering weight of his own fame, and the overt hostility of opponents and some teammates, who were in league over their envy and scorn for him. The 23-year-old blond, blue-eyed Stanford graduate was the poster boy for California Beautiful People, Athletes' Division. He had defied the NFL, refusing to play for the Baltimore Colts, the team that had drafted him. Then, after signing a $5 million contract with the Denver Broncos, he proclaimed his desire to win five Super Bowl rings, one for each finger.

But he barely had a finger-hold on his brilliant future after eight games. By the end of his first season, he was a bonafide bust. By the end of his second, he was making far more money than progress.

As a lifelong Denver resident, I'd never seen an athlete of Elway's magnitude —

other than the Denver Nuggets' David Thompson — come to town with more plausible hype. He could have gone over the wall when his career started crumbling, as Thompson had, in his own self-destructive way.

Yet Elway went the other way by playing football like a back-up tackle, not a halo-ed quarterback. During high school scrimmages, his coaches wanted him to wear a red vest that alerted defenders not to hit him. "There were always arguments," ex-teammate Darryl Stroh recalled. "It would make John go crazy. He hated the thing. He wanted to take it off. He'd scream: 'Hit me, hit me.' He hated to be special. He wanted to get into play and take his knocks."

Not much has changed. Over the years, I've seen Elway launch himself like a missile to gain a routine first down at midfield during a game that meant little. I've seen him throw diving blocks to clear the way for his running backs, for little visible gain. I've seen him bitterly scold himself for a mediocre pass — in practice.

John Elway is a player.

For this sportswriter, that's more than passing praise.

Elway can throw a football **40** yards at bullet speed and **60** yards with cross-hair accuracy. One of his passes tore the flesh off a finger of a Stanford receiver, exposing the bone.

Chapter One — The Arm

AFTER A GLOOMY DEFEAT IN 1995, THE DENVER BRONCOS had nothing left to do but count the bodies. The injuries had been piling up for weeks, and even John Elway sounded as if he might become a casualty of another dying season.

In a weary monotone following a loss to the Kansas City Chiefs, which kept the team out of the playoffs for the second consecutive season, the graying, ashen-faced quarterback talked openly about retirement.

Eventually, however, Elway was stopped in his tracks by one of the NFL's most durable and enduring legends: himself.

Although his numbers already made him suitable for framing in Canton, Ohio, Elway decided to continue to play the game of his life. Before he's finished, Elway hopes to pass and run for more yardage than any quarterback in NFL history, including Johnny Unitas, Dan Marino, Fran Tarkenton, Joe Montana, — and Bobby Layne, one of Elway's enduring role models.

During the past two decades, Elway has gone from blue jeans to power ties, frat boy to international icon, All-American letterman to filigreed businessman. But on the field, he's still the same ol' John, burning with timeless passion to run and pass and tackle any obstacle that stands in the way of winning, even if it means diving headfirst into a muddy end zone or lifting his fist in defense of a fallen buddy.

In an era of bejeweled narcissists and baleful outlaws, Elway is a football fundamentalist who missed only 10 starts in his first 14 seasons because of injuries; won more games than any starter in NFL history; led the Broncos out of the pocket of doom to victory with innumerable fourth quarter, game-saving drives; and, in an era of wandering stars, played in one city for one team, like the passing stars of old.

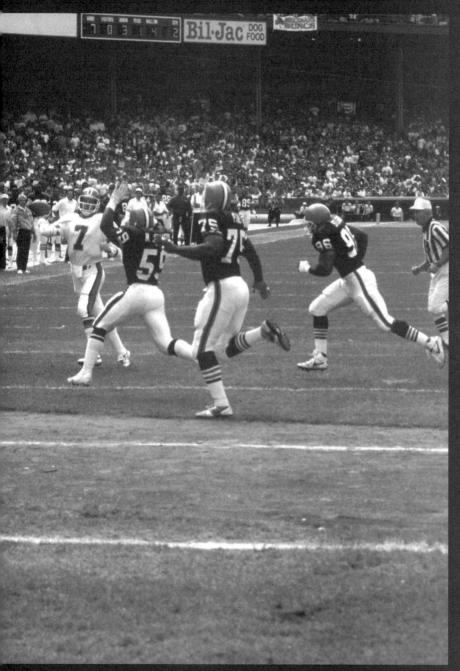

Elway is a defense's worst nightmare when he's on the run, scanning the field for a receiver. "He was the only quarterback we were ever told not to chase from the pocket," said former Cleveland and Oakland defensive lineman Bob Golic.

Moreover, Elway has survived countless surgeries, hundreds of sacks, a controversial showdown with the NFL, a harrowing rookie season, three humiliating Super Bowl defeats, devoted critics, the withering burden of a coach (Dan Reeves) with whom he couldn't communicate, as well as his own ruthless perfectionism.

But Elway armed himself for the long run with the loyal help of his father, a college coach, and his own right arm, which just happens to be the most dangerous in the game's history.

"John Elway is the Michael Jordan of the NFL," Joe Theisman said. "You expect every one of Jordan's shots to go in the basket and you expect every one of John's passes to be something special."

Added Joe Namath: "Everyone should realize that John is special. We might not have seen anyone quite like him before."

Elway's arm doesn't look that powerful.

It's 34 inches long. The biceps are a modest 12 inches unflexed. The forearm is unformidable looking. The wrist is inconspicuous. The hand could belong to an average quarterback.

But only Elway can throw a football 40 yards at bullet speed, 60 yards with cross-hair accuracy, 70 yards with a tight spiral — while backpedaling — and 80 yards on a powerful whim. Only Elway can fire a 66 mph fireball, 50 yards downfield — and 30 cross-field; or tear the flesh off a receiver's finger; or stamp an X on a receiver's chest with the point of the ball.

All great quarterbacks have signature assets. Joe Montana was the master of timing and precision. John Unitas had perfect form; Sonny Jurgensen was the best pure passer; no one could see the field better than Dan Fouts; Dan Marino has the quickest release since Joe Namath; Bobby Layne threw an ugly pass but won nonetheless.

Elway?

His arm is his destiny.

It's carried him through good times, bad times and mad times — on fields richly grained with history and ancient blood — and to AFC Championships, Super

Elway's signature play is the one in which he sprints to one sideline, stops, scans, pivots, and then throws a rope to the far side. "I used to strain every muscle in my body to throw 70 yards, and he stands there and flicks his wrist," former Cleveland Browns great Otto Graham said.

Bowls and hundreds of NFL and college games.

It's enabled him to pass for tens of thousands of yards and hundreds of touchdowns in the NFL, to break defenses into ungatherable fragments, to make hyperbole plausible for normally underwhelmed critics.

It was generations in the making, too.

John's grandfather, Harry Elway, quarterbacked a 1908 Pennsylvania team that played against Jim Thorpe, one of the century's greatest athletes. John's father, Jack Elway, was a star freshman quarterback at Washington State, before an injury ended his career.

He passed his skills to his son, who passed 'em into history.

"I've been blessed with a gift from God for throwing a football," John said.

In high school, John's knee almost buckled and snapped during the first half of a Friday night game. At halftime, he was forced to limp to the dressing room. But after a doctor wrapped his knee, Elway headed right back into the action.

In the second half, Elway "hopped" to his left on a roll-out, which bought him enough time to locate a receiver streaking to the end zone 60 yards away.

Despite his injury, which forced him to rely almost entirely on his arm, Elway fired a perfect scoring strike.

The stadium went eerily silent, before a roar arose from the part of a crowd that 16-year-olds rarely touch.

"I used to strain every muscle in my body to throw 70 yards, and he stands there and flicks his wrist," former Cleveland great Otto Graham said.

One day, after a Granada Hills practice, Elway stood at the 10-yard line, a teammate at the 50. When his friend threw the ball on a long arc, John knocked it from the sky with a smart bomb. Another time John and his buddies headed to the 35, where they took turns trying to strike an upright with a pass. John hurled perfect strikes.

When Stanford's punter skipped a practice, Elway saved the day by "throwing" punts that sailed as high as real ones. They came down like missiles. Elway's father warned: "Don't turn your arm loose" — for show. But that didn't stop John from a little visual imaging.

"I think I could throw (a baseball) out of the Stanford ball park," Elway said during his college days. "It's 335 feet down the line. Everybody has their own security thing. My arm is mine. I have great confidence in it."

Because of his armed might, Elway can deliver the ball into a fast-closing spot, or into the best spot for a receiver to catch it. He can wait an extra second or two before releasing the ball — which is often enough to set a receiver free. And he can do it falling down, getting up, lying down, off one foot, off the wrong foot and against all odds and defenses.

In 1985, Elway spotted receiver Vance Johnson seven yards downfield, and 25 yards cross-field. Oakland Raiders' cornerback Lester Hayes was a step or two away, in perfect position to pounce, until Elway zapped it by him.

"I didn't even see the ball," Hayes said. "I barely saw the blur. He nailed me. Elway is unstoppable. He's done things I've never seen before, and I've got lots of film."

"He's the most dangerous because he has the ability to run to his left and throw the ball back to his right with a lot of mustard on it," ex-Raiders cornerback Mike Haynes said. "When he's running to his right, he can throw it 60 yards on one foot."

During his Stanford days, in the face of a massive Southern Cal pass rush, Elway was running to save his head while simultaneously searching for a receiver.

"I was in deep, deep trouble," he said.

Elway ran to his left, reversed field, then veered to his left again.

"He has the instincts to move around as well as anybody in the game," Fran Tarkenton said. "When I came in I was a freak because I could move around. People said, 'You can't win with a quarterback running out of the pocket.'"

Then it happened.

In blurring succession, Elway planted his feet, cocked his hips, opened up his shoulders, snapped his right shoulder back, and released a missile that traveled

72 yards in the sweet California air for a touchdown.

"He was the only quarterback we were ever told not to chase from the pocket," former Cleveland and Oakland defensive lineman Bob Golic said. "He's actually more dangerous when you have him on the run. When he's scrambling and on the run, it just accentuates the power of that gun of his. And it all starts with that gun."

In 1991, with the score tied 16-16, Elway faced third and 17 from his 17-yard line, as time wound down against Kansas City. He rolled to his right, stopped, faced the opposite sideline, then arced a pass to Mark Jackson that went through the Chiefs like an arrow. As the Broncos kicked the game-winning field goal, press box math whizzes calculated the ball had traveled 43 yards downfield, and 43 yards across field, and, when all the figuring was done, 71 yards in all.

"He's extremely well-trained," former Green Bay quarterback Bart Starr said. "He makes great use of his legs. I've been impressed when he's had to scramble and then he has to come to a position of throwing. When he's rolled out and regained his position, that's when you see the fundamentals come into play, because he seldom overstrides. And it's easy to overstride, after all that moving. But he comes back into control and regains that rhythm."

In 1996, at age 36, Elway was caught in the middle of Oakland's antic pass rush. Defensive end Pat Swilling grabbed him, but Elway spun 180 degrees and into open sight of a receiver. Then, realizing Swilling had fallen to the turf in the other direction, he spun 180 degrees to come full circle. In a flash, he saw Shannon Sharpe in the back of the end zone. The passage from Elway to Sharpe was too narrow for breathing, but Elway shot a magic bullet straight to Sharpe's heart.

"John Elway is the master of the inconceivable pass thrown to the unreachable spot," Fox analyst Pat Summerall said.

Tell the Washington Redskins about it. In 1995, on a dying September day, the Broncos were breaking down. With six seconds remaining, and the score tied 31-31, Denver had the ball on Washington's 43-yard line, facing fourth and 10. It was a time to pause and think, but Elway wasn't in a thinking mood. He was mobilizing. Almost out of habit, he stepped back to midfield, stepped away from on-rushing trouble, then reached back into his pocketful of miracles and produced a pass that sailed into the end zone and Rod Smith's uplifted hands.

While the Redskins staggered around with home-from-the-war stares, Elway swaggered into the Broncos locker room, like John Wayne in cleats.

"I wish I was still out there," he said an hour later.

He is — along with his golden arm.

"I wouldn't trade it for anything," Elway said. "From my youngest days, I always wanted to be the best. Fortunately, I've been blessed with this arm, plus a coach telling me what to do. My dad."

Elway doesn't even need to be planted to throw one of his long strikes. "When he's running to his right, he can throw it 60 yards on one foot," ex-Raiders cornerback Mike Haynes said.

When Elway was traded to the Broncos, the city was electrified. His feats at Stanford were common knowledge to all Broncos fans, who immediately began planning for some Super Bowls. Elway was one of the few sophomore quarterbacks ever to earn All-American honors.

Chapter 2 — Father, Son and the Wonder Years

JACK ELWAY WAS ENRAGED IN 1981 AS HE WATCHED HIS SON stagger through the blackest day of his college career. John, a Stanford junior, completed only six of 24 passes for 72 yards, threw five interceptions and was sacked seven times.

Even worse, a sprained ankle made him a tempting target for even bloodier hits.

As angry as he was, Jack could do nothing to stop it. He coached John's opponent, San Jose State, but he couldn't tell his blitzing linebackers to take it easy on his son — not on their best day. Underdog San Jose State stunned Stanford with a 28-6 victory. But as father and son walked tearfully together out of Stanford Stadium, Jack was fuming because the Cardinal's coaches hadn't removed John from harm's way.

"How did I feel?" said the elder Elway, his hands shaking as he drank a Pepsi. "As a father, I'm not very goddamm happy. John was obviously injured. He showed great courage."

Jack Elway's will to win is nearly viral. So is John's. But their need for one another is even stronger. Over three decades, Jack created some imposing teams from the raw material of youth. But John is his ultimate masterpiece.

For purists, Elway is a throwback to classic quarterbacks from the golden past like Johnny Unitas and Bobby Layne, whose will and wit and warrior spirit still enrich the game. They see Johnny Elway and they really see Johnny U. or Detroit's compulsively competitive Layne.

That isn't a coincidence.

Elway was taught to pass and run and lead by his dad, who used Layne as one of his prototypes.

But no prototype ever prepared him for John's singular play. Or his signature play — the one in which John sprints to one sideline, stops, scans, pivots, and then throws a 60-yard rope to the far side.

"It combines all his strengths — the arm strength, scrambling skills, peripheral vision, instincts and the way he thrives under pressure — all in one play," Jack explains.

Jack's eyes get a distant look when he describes his son's ultimate play, as if staring at a priceless canvas that he himself has painted — which, in a sense, he has.

"He's the reason I am what I am today," John said.

Truth is, John nearly became history trying to make it.

At his first training camp, he felt like he'd journeyed from Palo Alto to Bedlam. By season's end, he'd become a bumbling parody of himself. After a couple seasons, the prevailing question about Elway was, "Whatever happened to him?"

The questions changed in ensuing years, but not the anguish level. Elway almost single-handily took the Broncos to Super Bowl XXI, but a 39-20 loss to the New York Giants depressed him; a 42-10 loss to Washington in Super Bowl XXII humiliated him; a 55-10 loss to the San Francisco 49ers in Super Bowl XXIV mocked him.

Elway saw with lucid misery that Joe Montana and Dan Marino were having the brilliant careers he was supposed to have.

In 1989, Elway blew a gasket, saying, "I'm about to suffocate," from his fishbowl life in Denver. He fumed about coach Dan Reeves' offense, which suffocated his once-in-a-generation talents.

The NFL was eating his heart.

But during the darkest days, all of John Elway's energy was closed like a fist around one thing: football.

Football and family.

Jack Elway doubles — or rather quadruples — as father, confidant, guardian and heat shield.

The elder Elway armed his protégé — and prodigy — with the emotional, as well as tactical and physical weapons, to withstand the assaults of fate, 300-pound linemen, and even 160-pound columnists.

"Being a coach's son has helped me in so many ways, physically, mentally, technique-wise," John said. "My dad is my best friend, my confidant. There have been many, many, many, many times I thought I was losing my sense of humor. It was so hard at times. But I always looked at it like it was something I wanted to pay the price for. I always went out and challenged myself to be as good as I can be.

"That's the way I was taught. He was always there when it got so tough. I could always talk to him. He was always there to help."

Father-son duos are a familiar part of football lore.

Marv Marinovich raised his baby to be an NFL quarterback with the cerebral detachment of a research scientist. He began stretching Todd's hamstrings when he was one-month old, and designed an exercise regimen by the time he could crawl.

Todd was certainly the only kid on his block — and perhaps America —who turned 18 without ever having tasted a Big Mac, Fritos or Twinkies. His father forbade junk food.

At friends' birthday parties, Todd took his own cake and ice cream — without sugar and refined white flour. By the time Todd was in school, he had a battalion of experts working with him on quickness, speed, peripheral vision, throwing motions, body control, mind … seven days a week. He made it to Southern Cal, and was a first-round draft pick of the Raiders. But amid allegations of drug use and declining interest, Todd's football career crumbled before he could reach the destiny his father had fixed for him.

"I wish I could go somewhere else and be someone else," he said during his USC days. "I don't want to be Todd Marinovich."

Archie Manning, one of the greatest quarterbacks of his era, may see his son

Peyton become the greatest of his era. Archie nurtured and developed Peyton's talents with a benign and sometimes humorous touch.

Archie came home from New Orleans Saints practices every day and organized games for his two sons and their neighborhood buddies. He filmed many with his camcorder, pretending they were being broadcast on national TV, even to the point of simulating pre-game introductions.

After Saints' home games, Manning's sons played on the Superdome field. As they became more serious about their games, Archie did as well, offering increasingly sophisticated X's and O's advice.

But Jack Elway could write the ultimate book on raising a quarterback.

In 1957, at his parents' home in Hoquiam, Washington, Jack gave an engagement ring to Janet, his bride-to-be, with one request. "Give me a baby boy."

On June 28, 1960, in Port Angeles, Washington, Janet gave him twins; John and Janna, joining sister Lee-Ann, born 18 months before. Janna played tennis at Stanford, and then became a teaching pro in the San Francisco area. Lee-Ann, is a lifelong sports fan.

"I like to tell people I got married, had a honeymoon for 18 months, and then all hell brook loose the next 18," Jack said. "But having the twins was such a thrill, and all of the kids, being so close to the same age, developed a special bond. Even as little kids, I can remember John crawling on the floor by himself, and looking around to see where Janna was and crawling right over to her. And then the two of 'em would start jabbering at each other in that special language twins have."

The Elway children grew up in the nomadic ways of a football coach, migrating through three states and six towns as Jack worked his way up to a job at a major university.

"We lived from Saturday to Saturday, our emotions riding on a football game," Jack said.

Elway was head coach at Port Angeles (Wash.) High School and Gray Harbor (Wash.) Community College (1961-66), and served in assistant roles at Montana (1967-71) and Washington State (1972-75). Then it was on to Cal

State Northridge (1976-78), San Jose State (1979-83) and Stanford (1984-88), where he made his mark as a head coach with creative, multi-dimensional offenses.

Before joining the Broncos scouting department, he also coached the Frankfurt Galaxy in the World League (1991-92).

Like most coaches, Jack was often only a visitor in his own home, leaving early in the morning and returning late at night during the season. When the recruiting season began, he was on the road more than not, and not until that phase was over could he finally settle into home life like a hammock.

With his rumpled clothes — someone once said he looked like an unmade bed — and weathered face, the chain-smoking Elway resembles actor Walter Matthau, with the dry wit to match.

During his trying tenure at Stanford, the elder Elway wrote a weekly column for a local paper, gently mocking himself and the school's pretensions.

"I am still in search of the Stanford Image," he wrote. "I first thought maybe it had something to do with the clothes you wear. I had to admit I thought Brooks Brothers were a couple linebackers for USC."

With Stanford's rigid academic standards, Elway had to work harder than most just to recruit a core of quality players. In 1985, he traveled to the homes of 75 recruits, from Oregon to Florida to New York, using his humor and the instincts of a politician — his brother was a state representative and congressional candidate — to close the sale.

"Survival is the only real goal I've had," he said.

Elway didn't do that at Stanford. He was fired in 1988, which embittered John, who now says he should have played for his father at San Jose State rather than for the Cardinal.

But Jack made all the shrewd moves with John, whose passion for sports needed retaining walls.

He started John in kindergarten a year later than normal so he'd have a more fully developed body by high school. When John picked up a plastic bat and assumed his natural right-handed stance, Jack immediately converted him into a left-handed hitter in a pre-emptive strike against curveballs. He wouldn't let him ski in Montana's mountains, although his sisters did. If John didn't become a star athlete, it wasn't going to be because of a skiing accident.

He convinced him to play quarterback instead of halfback. When Jack became Cal State Northridge's head coach, he scouted the L.A. area for a high school with a high-tech passing attack. And as the 1983 NFL draft neared, Jack helped John play the baseball card against the Baltimore Colts. By threatening to sign with the New York Yankees, who had employed him the previous summer on their Class A team, the Elways triggered a trade to Denver.

But Jack couldn't control one crucial development.

"I didn't have any idea how big he was going to be," Jack said. "He wasn't very big until ninth grade. He was slender, 5-8, but he really had a growth spurt from ninth grade on. Entering his junior year he was 6-1 and he spurted up another inch-and-a-half and that took him to 6-3 at college. Then he grew about an inch in his freshman year at Stanford, so that took him to about 6-4. "

During the Wonder Years, John and Jack were wonderful friends.

The images are everywhere in the Elways' memories: Seven-year-old John on the sideline, alone, watching his dad's team practice, despite incessant rain; John pleading for another game of one-on-one in the driveway, despite a fading sun and gathering chill. "One more time, one more time"; John listening in rapt awe as his father and his colleagues held a post-game post-mortem; Jack and John on a baseball field on an August afternoon, exchanging horsehide tales and ancient banter. "We have the bases loaded and two out," said Jack, in his best Mel Allen voice. "It's the bottom of the ninth in the seventh game of the World Series, and the whole season rides on the shoulders of the next batter. Can he do it?"

"Yes, yes," John shouts back.

"Even then, John had an ability to concentrate on details and go after it," Jack said. "He learned early on the difference between winning and losing. He found he liked winning a hell of a lot better."

John made his football debut in fourth grade, as a running back for the Little Grizzlies of Missoula. Because of a conflict, his father missed much of the first half, then played catch-up with Montana basketball coach Jud Heathcote, who later coached Magic Johnson at Michigan State.

"What'd I miss?" he asked.

"Well, either every kid on that field is the worst football player I've ever seen, or your boy is the greatest player I've ever seen," Heathcote said.

By halftime, John, who ran through a pair of sneakers every month, had run for four touchdowns.

"When I was eight years old, my favorite player was Calvin Hill, a running back with the Dallas Cowboys," he said. "They were my favorite team then. I wore his number in Pee-Wee football and went around calling myself Calvin Elway."

But Little John was a quarterback at heart.

"I was always throwing things, mudballs, dirtclods. I'd set up bottles on a fence and knock 'em down all day."

John's arm was so powerful he switched to quarterback in junior high, with some prodding from his dad. Jack credits his wife's gene pool for much of John's success. "From her, he got the size — she's 5-9. The big hands. Whatever good looks he's got. Some of my close friends look at me and ask me how I produced a son like that, and I just tell them I was an overachiever when I got married.

"But he got the arm from me," Jack added.

Jack revealed his ultimate dreams for his only son when he filled out a question-naire about him for the Dallas Cowboys, for whom he was a part-time scout. Although John was only 12 at the time, Jack, in a stroke of whimsy, wrote: "He's 6-2, 185 pounds, has a good arm, good speed, good agility. But he has a bad attitude because he didn't clean the swimming pool."

Actually, John had little time for anything except sports, even during the summer, when his schedule of baseball, basketball and football camps and contests tested his parents' aptitude for time and stress management. During the Wonder Years, the Elways took just one family vacation, and even that requires an asterisk, since Jack drove his son to and from a distant baseball camp each day. Why not? The results were invariably positive.

At Washington State's basketball camp, John, a ninth-grader, caught the eye of

Jack Elway knew his son was special by his junior year in high school, when he led Grand Hills High to a last-second victory. "What a competitor," Jack said.

Cougars coach George Raveling. "George said if John was going into football he was going into the wrong sport," the elder Elway recalled.

Raveling fired off a telegram to Elway before Super Bowl XXI: "Dear Shotgun: Congratulations on your great season. Best of luck in the Super Bowl. I still think you should have played basketball."

"John was always so involved in sports," his mother said. "About all we ever did was go to different sporting events. There were a few nights in Missoula when it was so cold I couldn't even get the dogs to go with me to pick up John — much less one of the girls."

Janet is a traditional coach's wife. She had to console and prepare her children for each move and new school, in addition to all the normal duties of running a house and raising three children. She was the one who drove John to a junior high basketball game, sat in the cold bleachers, then drove home, all the while wondering whether the car battery would last. She was the one who had to calm the house after her son or husband lost a game.

"John inherited my total inability to adjust to the depression and pain that comes with losing," Jack said.

Janet also had to deal with the fans who screamed insults at her husband or son from the safety of the stands.

"She's always been kind of an intense fan," John once told the *Denver Post*. "And she's never been afraid to tell anyone what she thinks. From what I've heard from my sisters, she told a few people to shut their mouths when she thought they were getting on me for no good reason."

In 1976, Jack took his first college head coaching job at Cal State Northridge. The timing was good, since John was entering high school. Jack was able to scour the Southern California area for a football team that threw 40-50 times a game. He hit gold at Granada Hills High School, and quickly found a nearby home.

The Elways' moves were always choreographed with one another's interests in mind. When John was pondering scholarship offers, his only real decision was between USC and Stanford because of his desire to remain near his family. It was no coincidence that he enrolled at Stanford the same year his father became head coach at San Jose State. Palo Alto is 15 miles north on Highway 101 from San Jose, a drive the Elways made too many times to count.

But that was four years away. In 1976, Elway was far from being a franchise player. Granada coach Jack Neumeier's first memory of him is as a shy and skinny freshman. But soon he was throwing touchdown bombs with stunning regularity for the junior varsity team. After the varsity got off to an 0-3 start the next season, Neumeier made Elway his starter.

"I couldn't have come to a better program. We threw on almost every down," Elway said.

There were glitches. When an assistant hit his son, Jack went on the attack.

"I told the guy he could apologize now or meet me outside and get the (bleep) kicked out of him; or he could wait until John turned 21 and have him kick the (bleep) out of him," Jack said. "He apologized."

But overall, John's years at Granada Hills passed like a sweet dream.

During his junior season, Elway passed for 3,039 yards and led Granada to the Los Angeles city semifinals. He went to a new plateau in the San Fernando Valley, just over the Hollywood Hills, during the fading minutes of an L.A. city playoff game.

San Fernando had a remarkable running game, which Granada Hills couldn't stop, but San Fernando couldn't stop Elway's passing game either. With 1:30 left, San Fernando took a 35-33 lead, and Elway had to take over on his own 32-yard line, the weight of a season on his shoulders. Since Granada had a sophisticated audible system, Elway was able to ad-lib at the line of scrimmage. He quickly moved Granada downfield, and, then, with 20 seconds left, on a play called In-and-Out, he fired a scoring strike to Chris Sutton. But a holding penalty wiped out the touchdown, and the ball was moved back to the 9. Elway calmly called the same play, and scored again, lifting Granada to a 40-35 win.

"I wonder if he's as good as I think he is," Jack said to his wife as they left the stadium. "I wonder if John realizes just how good he can be."

By that point, Elway was leaving defenses in fragments with both his passing and running. One of Jack's first lessons to his son was, "Always be ready to run."

According to the classic mantra, drop-back passers must remain in the pocket, and take the heat or hit, rather than abandon it for who knows what.

But Jack Elway believed a quarterback should run often and hard, thus forcing a defense into a potentially paralyzing dilemma.

How do you defend against a quarterback who has the power to throw game-bending bombs at will, and the nimbleness to disappear in a puff of smoke from a tackler's grasp? What do you do when a quarterback can run with the speed and cunning of a halfback one moment, and throw a perfect dart the next — on the same seamless play?

Not much, if the quarterback is a first-rate passer and runner like Elway.

"Why is it that when experts talk about a 'complete' quarterback they never include running as part of the package?" he said. "Defenses don't account for the quarterback. Nobody does. So it becomes 11 men against 10. Running just puts the pressure back on the defense."

As his reputation grew, so did Elway's ambition and regard for his future.

After finishing his homework each evening, he spent an extra hour studying game film and memorizing new plays. In the summer, while friends headed to the beach, Elway threw 300 passes per day. In practice, he used a stop watch to make sure he dropped back and set up in the same amount of time. By doing so, he knew where his receivers were before he looked up, saving time and grief.

At first glance, Elway might appear to be "The Natural," a rare athlete who prospers by sheer fluid physical superiority. In truth, Elway is an anxious perfectionist who agonizes over a solitary mistake — even in practice.

John stayed focused in school, as well. Although math was his favorite subject, he ran into a brick wall in geometry. He couldn't grasp the relationship between numbers and shapes, but he managed to pass, thanks to intensive cramming. At Stanford, despite all the demands on his time and attention, he earned a degree in economics, with a 3.0 grade-point average. And true to his grinder's ways, Elway literally slept with his play book — and watched hundreds of hours of game film — after his troubling rookie NFL season.

Elway left no detail to chance entering his senior season at Granada High.

Physically and emotionally, he was ready for his ultimate season.

"I told him we were going to go for 4,000 yards, shatter the national record," Neumeier told the *Rocky Mountain News* before the 1986 Super Bowl.

But in Week Four, after throwing for 1,837 yards, Elway crumpled to the turf. His season was over.

"He was rolling out in the first half and it — the left knee he had hurt playing basketball — just popped," Neumeier said. "Nobody even hit him.

"My heart just went through the ground. I didn't even want to go to practice after that. It just about killed me."

Elway underwent knee surgery, went through rehab, and for the first time, tried to imagine his life without football. He couldn't.

The following spring, Elway compensated for his stunted football season in baseball. He was voted Southern California Player of the Year, thanks in large part to his performance in the L.A. city championship game against Crenshaw, which featured future major-leaguers Darryl Strawberry and Chris Brown.

Elway, who hit .419 that season, played third base. But after Crenshaw scored three runs in the third inning to take a one-run lead, he was summoned to the mound.

"I hadn't considered that I might pitch because I hadn't pitched in five to six weeks," he said. "I threw them nothing but fastballs. I've never thrown a curveball because I didn't want to hurt my arm. Strawberry hit a couple deep ones, but he never got around."

In fact, Strawberry was 0-for-4, Brown 0-for-3, and Crenshaw, 10-4 losers, managed just one hit in all against Elway, whose fastball was once clocked at 93 mph.

Elway managed to have some fast times as well at Granada High — at least by "American Graffiti" standards. After the big game, he and his buddies cruised the boulevards of the San Fernando Valley in Elway's 1964 tan Buick LeSabre, routinely making pit stops at Bob's Big Boy or the Pizza Parlor.

Near the end of their high school adventures, Elway and Co. got a 12-by-12 block of ice, loaded it on the roof of the LeSabre, and headed to a nearby golf course. On the top of a 65-foot hill, they stuck a towel on the ice, hopped on, and slipped into the night.

When Elway arrived at Stanford, he was the All-American Boy, circa 1955: blond, blue-eyed, graceful in a muscular way, adored by fawning fans, respected by his large contingent of easy-going, beer-gulping buddies, and eager to do right by everybody.

He dated a blonde named Janet Buchan, a nationally recognized swimmer, whom he married a year out of college. On their first date, John and Janet played catch with a football - until she broke a finger trying to handle one of his passes.

Elway lived in a 9-by-9 frat-house room with a giant water bed and little else beyond a couple posters. This third-floor enclave was paradise for Elway, who reveled in the classic squalor and breezy camaraderie of college life, "Animal-House" style.

"That's all I want to be — one of the boys," Elway said.

After Elway signed a $5 million contract with the Denver Broncos, he hurried back to his fraternity house, and one last blast from a rapidly receding past.

"Hey Elwood," a frat brother said when he returned. "When'd you get back?"

"Last night," Elway said.

"Did you sign?"

"Yeah."

"Denver?"

"Yeah?"

"Congratulations. You got third-floor bathroom duty this week."

"OK."

"It's frustrating for (reporters)," said former Stanford sports information director Bob Rose. "They come wanting to do the ultimate John Elway story, and all they find is a very simple guy who isn't hiding anything. Just a nice kid who has a chance to be the best quarterback to ever play the game."

Even during his Stanford days, Jack remained Elway's closest friend and confidant. So why didn't John play for San Jose State?

"There are nights, after I've had about three vodka martinis, when I'll say to myself, 'Jack, old boy, you've got to be the dumbest sumbitch in this whole world. You have the best quarterback in America across the breakfast table from you and you let him get away."

"I know that if I said, 'John, come with me to San Jose State,' he would've come but that wouldn't have been fair to him."

In truth, Elway had been eyeing Stanford for years, so the 59 other schools that offered him scholarships — apart from USC — received just passing consideration, as did the Kansas City Royals, who selected him with a latter pick of the major league baseball draft.

The first week of Stanford practice Elway sent two quarterback prospects packing. Babe Laufenberg and Grayson Rogers transferred to other schools — Laufenberg to Indiana and Rogers to the University of Pacific — where they both became starters.

Turk Schonert, a senior who was drafted by the Cincinnati Bengals, survived Elway's challenge and led the nation in passing. But Elway still managed to play in nine games, finishing sixth in Pac-10 passing efficiency. He made his mark on the practice field as well, as he would in ensuing years. Wide receiver Don Lonsinger saw an Elway pass tear his outstretched hand, cutting his finger badly enough to leave a bone exposed.

Elway blossomed during his first season as a starter, when he became one of the few sophomore quarterbacks ever to earn All-America honors. He set Pac-10 records for touchdown passes, completions, touchdowns — both running and passing — and total offense (2,939 yards), plus a single-game mark for TD passes (six against Oregon State) and TD passes in one quarter (four, also against the Beavers).

After he threw for three touchdowns and ran for another during Stanford's shocking 31-14 upset of Oklahoma, Sooners coach Barry Switzer said, "John

Elway put on the greatest exhibition of quarterback play and passing I've ever seen on this field."

Elway's junior season, however, was a different matter. The Cardinal lost to Purdue (27-19), Ohio State (24-19), Arizona (17-13), Southern Cal (25-17), Arizona State (62-36), Washington (42-31) and, hardest of all, to San Jose State (28-6).

A couple days before the Elway Civil War, which remained predictably civil, John and Jack appeared together at a football writers' luncheon in San Francisco. "I've been a fan of my dad's all my life. But when it comes down to this game, I have to be selfish. Last year, no kidding, dad gave me San Jose's first play of the game, a quarterback draw. I told Coach Harbaugh (Stanford defensive coordinator Jack Harbaugh) what it was going to be and he said, 'yeah, sure.' Well it was a quarterback draw and the coach and I just looked at each other. This year, I don't know if I can trust the old man."

Jack responded with a typical quip: "Sure I'll tell him the play when I know it. That's what makes us so effective. We never know what we're doing on offense."

In truth, the week leading up to the game was hellish.

"It's hard on the whole family," John told *Sports Illustrated*, "particularly my mother. It's Dad's job, after all and the family has always been centered around him. The thing is a whole lot worse for us than people think."

San Jose State's 28-6 victory was one of the elder Elway's career highlights. But in Jack's ultimate moment, John was dazed and bloodied from a bad beating. When his mother saw him, she burst into tears.

"We're all confused," Jack's wife said. "It's a terrible, wrenching experience."

Privately, Jack bitterly criticized the Stanford coaches for subjecting his son to continued abuse. Later he learned John had insisted on playing.

Throughout that hard fall, John was hobbled by a sprained right ankle, a chipped bone in his left hand and a mild concussion. When healthy, Elway was unstoppable. During two one-half quarters of a 63-9 win over Oregon State, for example, he completed 15 of 20 passes for 245 yards and three touchdowns.

But more often than not, he played with pain, especially over Stanford's mounting losses. The team finished with a 4-7 record — its worst since 1963. The Cardinal running game was ineffectual at best, and near the end, Elway argued with offensive coordinator Jim Fassel some days, and withdrew into silence others. "Until we won a few at the end, John was being consumed by his own competitive instincts," Fassel said.

Nevertheless, Elway completed 585 of his passes for 2,674 yards and 20 touchdowns, and never lost confidence in his own skills. "(He) believes if all else fails, he can always drop back and save us all with a long pass," wide receiver Mike Tolliver said.

In 1982, Elway led Stanford to a 43-41 win over the number-one ranked Washington Huskies and finished second to Herschel Walker in Heisman Trophy voting. His 24 touchdowns were the most by any quarterback in the country. His 3,242 passing yards earned him unanimous All-America honors.

But Elway had grown weary of shoot-outs. At one point during his college career, he asked Jack how Stanford could beat UCLA.

"Score 35 points," Jack said.

Stanford did; UCLA scored 38.

During the Elway years, Stanford didn't play in a bowl game. It should have. On Nov. 20, 1982, with California leading 19-17 and time fading, Elway drove Stanford on what appeared to be a game-winning drive. With four seconds remaining, Stanford's Mark Harmon kicked a 35-yard field goal to lift the Cardinal to a 20-19 lead.

On the ensuing kickoff Cal's Kevin Moen fielded the ball on the 43 and ran out the clock — at least that's what the Stanford band assumed as it poured onto the field. But at the same time, Moen ran 10 yards, lateralled the ball to Richard Rodgers, who was following him on the left sideline. He passed midfield and then shoved the ball back to Dwight Graner, who took it to the Stanford 44, where he was hit but lateralled the ball back to Richard Rodgers.

At the 48, Rodgers had the ball. He then lateralled it back to Mariet Ford at the Stanford 46.

Suddenly, there was running room for Ford, who made it to the 25-yard line, where some Cardinal waited. In desperation, he blindly threw the ball over his shoulder. Kevin Moen, the player who had fielded the kickoff, plucked it out of mid-air and raced toward the end zone.

Cardinal players tried to tackle him, but they had to deal with the Stanford band, which now came into play. Moen used oboe players and drummers and saxophonists as screens, then knocked over a trombone player and barged into the end zone.

What actually happened on this circus-like play? Nothing illegal, officials ruled. The touchdown stood. California won 25-20 in one of the strangest conclusions to any athletic event in American sports history.

Elway was full of rage and storm.

"That was one of the most unpleasant times of all," he said. "It was a game the refs lost total control of. That was always the biggest game on our schedule. That made it even tougher."

Elway's final Stanford stats were mind-numbing: 774 of 1,246 (62.1%), 9,349 yards, 77 touchdowns, 39 interceptions. But those were unconsoling facts for a quarterback who longed to go bowling on New Year's Day. He compensated in the diamond district. Yankees owner George Steinbrenner, in search of the next Mickey Mantle, thought he had found one in Elway, who turned Palo Alto into a mandatory stop on the scouting circuit.

"I see a lot of Mickey Mantle in him," Steinbrenner told *Sports Illustrated*. "We invited John to our Fort Lauderdale training camp. He got into the batting cage for the first time, and (batting coach) Mickey Rivers told him to bunt down the third-base line. He did. Told him to hit behind the runner, between first and second. He did. Same for second and third. Then he told him to hit it out of the park. He did."

Elway played right field in his freshman year at Stanford, and hit only .269. But he also had spring football. And besides, he had a good time.

"Standing out there in right field, it's a relief to know the whole world isn't revolving around me," he said.

After his tremendous sophomore football season, Elway entered the baseball season with invulnerable confidence. He hit .361 with nine home runs and 50 RBI in 49 games, and .444 in the NCAA Central Regionals, where he was a unanimous choice for the all-tournament team.

Elway, however, didn't play baseball at Stanford the following year, not with the Yankees now on the scene. In 1974, in an effort to protect multi-talented athletes from being raided by professional baseball teams, the NCAA began allowing them to be professionals in one sport and amateurs in all others. Knowing that Elway had two years of football ahead of him, and that he was the best pro quarterback prospect in the country, the Yankees drafted him in the second round of his sophomore season and signed him in the fall of his junior year with a $150,000 bonus. By signing him for one season, the Yankees simply preserved their draft rights, assuring that they would be the only major league team that could sign him.

It was a shrewd move on the Elways' part, because it gave them leverage in the NFL draft. By threatening to play major league baseball, John could avoid having to play for a bad team. In fact, insiders insist Elway never was serious about baseball; the point was to control his NFL fate.

During the summer of 1982 he played for the Yankees' New York-Pennsylvania Class A League team in Oneonta, N.Y. He could have played for any Yankee farm team, even a AAA one. "But they suggested (Oneonta, N.Y.) and that was fine for me. I knew I wouldn't be playing baseball for a year. I didn't want to go somewhere and flop."

But Elway did flop, at least at first. He opened the season June 18 in right field and didn't get his first hit until the third game. He was 3-for-27 in his first eight games, hitting .111 in the No. 3 or No. 4 spot.

His arm also tightened up.

"John felt that pressure of playing for money in Oneonta," Jack said. "He slumped, and he called me and said, 'Dad, I think my goal is to hit .100.' I told him to be aware of his mistakes but not to let them crush him."

Jack's word, as always, emboldened Elway, who ended his six-week stint with a .318 average, a team-leading 24 RBIs, and no errors in 42 games. In July, he hit .318

During the countdown for the draft, Elway insisted baseball was a serious option, which many regarded as a hollow ruse to avoid playing for the Baltimore Colts, who owned the first pick in the 1983 NFL draft.

"I love to take two steps into a fly ball and then hum it home, just let it fly and watch it move," he told *Sports Illustrated* as the draft neared. "There's no feeling like that. But then, throwing a football is a tougher release, a much harder thing to do. I'll just let them all do the wheeling and dealing, and then I'll decide. I know I can be happy either way. I won't look back."

The city of Baltimore itself was not the problem, the Elways later said. It was owner Robert Irsay — whom many considered impulsive and eccentric, and coach Frank Kush, an old-school autocrat and martinet. Jack Elway supposedly loathed him.

In fact, John never said publicly he wouldn't play for the Colts. But by insisting on playing in California, or perhaps Seattle, the message was crystal clear.

Besides, Kush knew from insiders that Elway was a mediocre baseball prospect. So from the start, the Colts' strategy was to demand the world in exchange for the top pick; or, failing that, take Elway and make the best possible deal afterward. The Raiders, San Diego Chargers and New England Patriots all made serious offers as draft day neared. In fact, the Raiders were on the verge of closing a deal, only to see it scuttled when the Chicago Bears, part of a potential three-way agreement, asked for Raiders defensive end Howie Long at the last moment. In 1983, Raiders owner Al Davis was in the middle of his lawsuit against the league, and the last thing the league wanted to see was Elway in a silver and black uniform.

By demanding Long, Chicago owner George Halas — acting in behalf of the NFL powers — made sure that wouldn't happen.

Elway was furious when Kush actually drafted him, and refused to accept his phone call.

Irsay entertained offers after the draft. But on May 2, six days after the draft, he ignored Kush's advice and sent Elway to Denver in exchange for offensive tackle Chris Hinton, a 1984 No. 1 pick, backup quarterback Mark Herrmann and $1 million. Hinton became a Pro-Bowl star, but in Denver the Elway deal remains the ultimate heist.

Elway, however, may have won the battle, but he lost the PR war.

"A spoiled, rich California brat," many said.

"He ought to grow up and pay his dues," Terry Bradshaw said.

Within months, Elway had collected 48 bags of hate mail.

Irsay exploited the backlash, saying "He'll never be any good ... We're going to get Elway. We signed a couple boys this week who are looking for Elway."

The Elway theatrics overshadowed another dramatic development. The Class of 1983 was a gold-mine for great quarterbacks. Six went in the first round, and four went on to become stars. The other two became starters at one point or another.

The first selected after Elway was Penn State's Todd Blackledge, who went to Kansas City with the seventh overall pick. With the 14th choice, Buffalo drafted Miami's Jim Kelly. New England followed immediately by taking Illinois' Tony Eason.

The New York Jets took Cal-State Davis' Ken O'Brien with the 24th pick, and Miami used the 27th spot to select Pittsburgh's Dan Marino, who had plummeted in scouts' ratings.

"I run out of superlatives when talking about John Elway of Stanford," New York Jets director of player personnel Mike Hickey said at the time. "He's the best I've seen since I've been scouting. When evaluating Elway, negatives are brought up that aren't negatives for most people. Elway is simply atypical — he has no weak points."

Marino and Elway will enter the Hall of Fame on the first ballot. Kelly, who led Buffalo to four Super Bowls, will join them shortly afterward.

O'Brien led the NFL in passing in 1985. Eason led New England to Super Bowl XX before injuries sapped his potential. The biggest disappointment was Blackledge, who never really succeeded as a starter.

In 1983, however, all that was light years away for Jack Elway.

He was thinking back to the day he was painting the family's house, which overlooked a school track in Missoula, when he heard over a loudspeaker that John had won a race. When John came home his father congratulated him, but John flew by him and up the stairs and into his room, slamming the door for angry punctuation. Janna had won the race, not John, who wasn't able to take defeat in stride.

"What a competitor," Jack said.

He was thinking about all their backyard games — the one-on-one baseball and basketball and football games — when John's apple-cheeked dreams colored their world.

"God he was fun."

And he was thinking back to the autumn Friday nights, when John would hurry home after a Granada Hills game, and then replay it for both of them.

"(I'd) talk over the whole game before I ever thought about going out with the boys," John said. "We'd just sit and talk."

There would be plenty of bad moments in the ensuing years, and brilliant ones, as well. But to Jack Elway, few topped the time his son spent with Bobby Layne.

"Bobby took John under his wings," Jack proudly says.

It was a symbolic moment for the Elways. Bobby Layne came before his time, but John's timeless play and ancient virtues made comparisons inevitable.

"I like the comparison with Layne because he was a tough guy. He wasn't just a quarterback. He was a football player," John said. "I'm not just a quarterback. I'm a football player."

In fact, the only thing Bobby Layne liked more than winning, was fighting to win. He'd give a foe an emotional and physical pummeling and revel in it. It's not a coincidence he was the last quarterback to play without a face mask. Heck, he would've played without a helmet.

On the eve of the final game of the 1962 season, Layne was dazed and bloodied from a minor car crash. Yet the blond, blue-eyed Texan played the next afternoon without thought, or second thought for that matter.

Alex Karras, Layne's friend and teammate, once hit a Chicago Bears offensive tackle with two sucker punches. He was moving in for the kill when the victim begged him to stop.

He was Karras' brother.

That's when Layne realized just how much he respected Alex Karras.

In his colorful book, *The Quarterbacks*, Mickey Herskowitz interviewed Layne about another butt-kickin' teammate, tackle Dick Stanfel.

"Once we were playing the 49ers," he said, "trying to get in for a score just before half. We ran a sweep to the sideline and Stanfel came back to the huddle, wheezing and hacking and out of breath. He's real hoarse and he mumbles to me, 'Bobbie, give me a time-out.'

"I was a real hardass about those things, you know, so I just said flat out, 'The hell with your time-out.' I called another play. Stanfel made his block and then he had to go off the field. The doctor looked at him and later diagnosed it. A broken back. Dick Stanfel made this block with a broken vertebra, and you know what I felt like, don't you, because the next day Dick was wearing a cast up to his neck."

Elway has a remarkable pain threshold, as well. By 1995, no quarterback had been sacked more and idled less.

"John is tougher than even linemen," Denver tight end Shannon Sharpe said. "Offensive linemen get banged around, but they don't get blind-sided. They don't get hit when it's unexpected. They know going into the game that they're going to get hit on every play. John knows he's going to get hit, but he doesn't know when. He's getting blindsided.

"Sometimes it just amazes me. He's lying on the ground, in obvious pain, but then he just picks himself up and calls the next play. He doesn't look for sympathy, he doesn't blame anyone, he doesn't look to the sideline to say, 'What's going on?' He just calls the next play."

Jack Elway isn't surprised.

"He stays in shape, plus he's been lucky as far as injuries," he said. "But there's another factor. He learned ... to stand up and take your licks in the pocket,

That's the way he was trained."

Elway goes out of his way to dive into the fray. Against the Minnesota Vikings a dozen years ago, he swaggered into the middle of a sprawling fight to defend his men.

Against the Los Angeles Raiders in 1988, despite a sprained thigh, bruised elbow and hyper-extended knee, Elway launched himself like a runaway missile toward the goal line.

Afterward, he probably had a beer with his linemen, his partners in grime.

"They play without getting headlines, because they love the game," he said. "I really respect them for that, and for their toughness. I admire toughness."

Like Elway, Layne was toughest in a tough spot.

The Lions' leader was in a giant jam in the 1953 NFL championship game against Cleveland. The Lions had the ball on their own 20, trailing 16-10, and Layne had three minutes to save the day. "Y'all block and ol' Bobby'll pass you right to the championship," Layne told his teammates, who saw him do just that.

Layne is considered the NFL's original Comeback Kid. Buddy Parker, his coach, introduced the two-minute offense, but Layne made it work.

"A real leader," Jack Elway said.

Like John.

Elway saved the day in the final seconds in a championship game against the Cleveland Browns — 33 years after Layne had pulled off the trick. Like Layne, Elway can play like a humbling parody of himself for three quarters, then suddenly see the light when it's about time to turn 'em out.

"He's got a real perception; he's always had the intangible thing, that power of observation, that awareness," Jack Elway said. "Being around coaches all his life, he got a real picture of what it takes to win, and of the atmosphere of a game. If he doesn't win, he suffers. He'll do anything to win.

"If I really thought about his most amazing day, I'd think about 'The Drive,' but

Bobby Layne. (© Detroit Lions)

I also might go back to the days when he was a Little Leaguer. Even then he had the toughness, the competitiveness, the drive, the love of football. I got to his first Little League game sort of late and he'd already scored four touchdowns."

The passion never dies in Elway, nor did it for Layne.

The Texas whiz kid came to his first NFL training camp by car, with his wife and college coach. At every stop for gas, the trio jumped out of the car, football in hand, and Layne's wife snapped the ball as he pivoted and went through all his moves. Layne's coach offered running commentary.

Years later, long after he'd retired, Layne wasn't in a retiring mood when it came to football.

"We looked forward to practice, we looked forward to games," he said. "We even looked forward to training camp. It was like going on vacation when we went to training camp. Guys got there early just to get up there and get their hands on the football. Today that spirit is gone."

Not with Elway.

In training camp, he still curses himself for blowing a play. After a loss, he still plunges into despair. After a win, he still beams. After all, he was taught to run, and throw and to play the game of his life with timeless grace and ancient passion — by a father who saw it all coming.

"The only reason he still plays is because he loves the game," said Vance Johnson, one of Elway's top receivers in the '80s and early '90s. "With all the money he's made, and all he's done, he has nothing to play for except for the love of the game.

"John Elway is a football player. That's all. He's an offensive lineman. He's the guy who runs downfield on kickoffs and makes the big tackle. He's a linebacker. He's a little bit of everything. He could've done anything he wanted to in the NFL. But he had a great arm, so he became a great quarterback."

Every day was media day when Elway arrived at his first training camp. Reporters from throughout the nation journeyed to Greeley to record his first days in the NFL. No item was too trivial for inclusion in the Elway Watch, including what he ate for lunch.

Chapter 3 — Breaking In

JOHN ELWAY'S BATTLE WITH BALTIMORE COLTS' OWNER Robert Irsay had been more malicious than anything he had prepared for, and he had prepared for a lot.

But now Elway bandaged his dreams, drew a new breath, and headed to training camp, where he could finally get down to the business of getting down to business.

He felt like getting down on his knees when it was over — in relief.

Training camp is every player's bane.

Persistent fatigue, broiling practice fields, grim dorms, overheated coaches — those are only some of the suffocating staples of this August NFL ritual, which sends shivers of dread through newcomers.

But not all of 'em.

On Day One Chicago Bears quarterback Jim McMahon strolled into coach Mike Ditka's office with an air of insolence and a can of Budweiser.

Ditka's response?

"I thought he was thirsty," he said.

Joe Namath responded with rote cool, too.

A reporter, trying to unnerve the New York Jets' new star, asked, "What was your major at Alabama, Joe, basket weaving?"

"No basket weaving was too tough," Namath replied, "so they put me in journalism instead."

That set the tone for Namath's jaunty rookie of the year season.

Elway, on the other hand, stumbled unwittingly into a storm center. After a press conference announcing his signing, the most-hyped rookie quarterback since Joe Namath told a club executive,

"Well, I'm glad this press stuff is all done with."

The executive started to laugh. Then tighten.

Over?

The show was just beginning, along with the unraveling of a star.

Coach Dan Reeves' impatience — and his decision to dumb-down the offense — hindered Elway's development. So did Elway's own impatience and anxiety. But the hurricane of media and fan scrutiny blew Elway away first.

"Everyone talked about the media in the Super Bowl, but it didn't compare with my rookie year," he said. "The toughest thing about my rookie year was the media. They wore me out."

There were menacing signs from the start — like the 53 media members who gathered in Greeley, a town of 60,000, 65 miles northeast of Denver.

On the first day, television cameras took pictures of newspaper photographers taking pictures of reporters interviewing Elway, who had a bird's eye view of the media bazaar. It took seven communication trailers to handle the throng of television and radio crews, creating a small forest of satellite dishes, antenna and bombast.

Nearly 30 reporters lived full-time in adjacent dorms. Most were local reporters chasing scoops, especially on Elway. *The Rocky Mountain News* and *Denver Post* battled daily in a bloody, bitter newspaper war that attracted national media attention in its own right. In Denver, every day was media day for Elway, and everything was fit to print for the Elway Watch, including fare such as:

"For the past two days, Elway has been wearing a pair of flowered shorts and a yellow T-shirt ... He is a devout follower of the soap opera "All My Children." ... He's a dollar richer, having won his bet with quarterback/wide receivers coach John Hadl on the USFL championship game. Elway had Philadelphia by six ... Elway (then single) danced with four women last night at ..."

Elway realized during his rookie season that he needed to add muscle to his lean body, and not just in his upper body. "I realized how important my mobility was to me. I knew I had to improve the strength in my legs."

"Every day, there was a front-page story on him," Hadl said. "I had never seen anything like it. Things like, 'Elway threw 97 passes in practice today ... two dropped, two overthrown.' It was ridiculous."

Elway was caught off guard when a *Post* reporter wrote he'd eaten peas and fried chicken at one particular lunch. The *News* insisted it was green beans. The reporters quibbled about it, before commencing the search for more sound bytes.

"We're past media hysteria," Broncos media director Jim Saccomano said. "We're long past hysteria."

Well, not quite.

Shortly after camp began, Elway needed to get a haircut, and the media wanted to document it. Saccomano was stuck in the middle, but this time he sided with Elway.

"He was doing so much for us, so I got hold of a barber, and he said he'd give him a haircut at his home. Then we found an off-duty Greeley policeman to pick up John in an unmarked police car, after the team meetings were finished, about 9:30 or so. So this guy picks him up, and takes him to the barber's house.

"The next morning John comes to practice and all the reporters are saying, 'He got a haircut!'"

After a couple weeks, the *News* asked its readers: "Is the media going overboard on coverage of Elway." One wrote back: "This poll proves you're going overboard."

"He is a freak show," Saccomano said.

Added ex-wide receiver Steve Watson: "John had the toughest first year of any player in the history of the game. It was ridiculous to subject a guy to that."

Not that fans — who lined up four deep to watch routine camp drills — resented the saturation coverage. To them, nothing succeeds like excess when it comes to the men in orange.

During the club's storied history, Denver has gone from cow town to uptown, laid back to high tech, suburbs to ex-urbs.

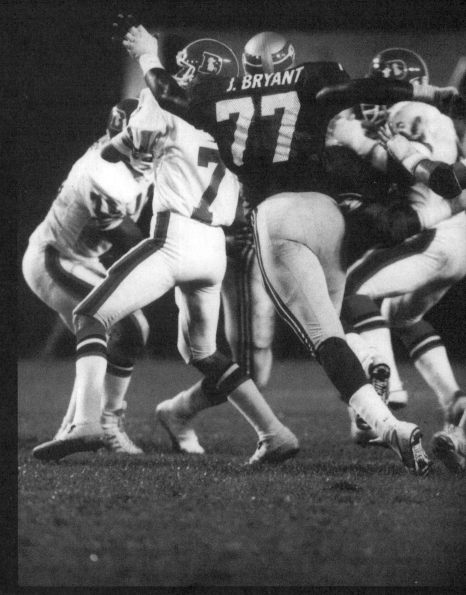

Elway lived up to all the hype in his first pre-season game against
Seattle. He entered the game in the fourth quarter to thunderous
approval, then completed five of six passes on a 10-play scoring drive.
"He's electric," said linebacker Tom Jackson.

But through changing times the Broncos remained a mass obsession of daunting dimensions. "When the Broncos win, we win. When they lose, we lose," a psychologist explained.

When the Broncos lose, some die.

After they fumbled five times during a 33-14 loss to Chicago in 1973, a gloomy fan shot himself in the head. "I've been a Broncos fan since they were first organized, and I can't stand the fumbling anymore," he wrote in a suicide note.

Some called that an heroic act.

During the 1977 Super Bowl season, the year acute Broncomania went epidemic, Rick Savage and his girlfriend entered a Denver bar for a few beers. Savage put a quarter in the juke box so he and his gal could dance.

Trouble was, everyone else wanted to watch the Broncos game, without distraction.

"Turn that crap off," a fan screamed at Savage.

Savage ignored him, so the man stalked to the juke box and killed the music. And then Savage.

"Nobody's going to mess with me when I'm watching the Broncos," he mumbled on his way to jail.

During the 1977 season, every fan did his part for the holy cause. In Denver, a convict asked the court to delay his move to another jail so he could watch a playoff game in familiar surroundings. In maternity wards, newborn babies were wrapped in orange swaddling clothes, and employees put "Super Bowl 78" stickers on cribs.

One Sunday there weren't enough shuttle buses to ferry fans to Mile High stadium. A woman left behind sued the bus company for $43 — the price of a season bus ticket. She won, and afterward the judge told her she could've asked for more money.

"That's the money I wanted," she said. "But what I really wanted was to see the Broncos."

As she left the court, the woman shouted, "We're No. 1."

In 1987, a 29-year-old woman drove into town, removed her clothes and rode an orange-painted horse through a downtown mall in exchange for two free tickets to a Broncos game. Another woman read an ad her husband had put in the paper, offering her in trade for a Super Bowl ticket. "He's dead meat," she said.

In 1987, the Cleveland-Denver AFC championship game attracted what is believed to be the largest share ever measured by the AC Nielsen and Co. — a 61 rating and 89 share.

At the height of the drama — the last hour of Denver's 23-20 victory — the game attracted a 65 rating/90 share. In other words, 90 percent of the TV sets in Denver were tuned to the game.

"I have never heard of a 90 share in a local market," a Nielsen spokesman said.

Perhaps fans were overcompensating for the team's early years, when the Broncos were best known for a cost-conscious general manager who wrestled fans for loose footballs; vertically striped socks, which eventually went up in flames during a public bonfire; and the fact they didn't post a winning record in their first 14 seasons.

After posting a 2-7 record, the strike-shortened year before, the Broncos needed Elway's help badly.

Veterans gathered en masse to watch the celebrated rookie at his first spring mini-camp.

After catching a perfectly thrown ball from Elway, Rick Upchurch showed him his preferred spot. It was Johnny on the spot the next play.

"I'm an idiot, and even I can tell he's super," quipped an assistant trainer.

Nevertheless, Elway found himself in a strange new world in Greeley. His No. 1 fear was "not being treated like one of the boys in Denver. I don't want to be like some guys I've seen — guys who are conceited and not well-liked. And I'd hate to go someplace and have dinner and then have someone come up to me and ask for an autograph. It more embarrasses me than makes me feel good."

Needless to say, Elway was shocked by real life in the NFL, where veterans hold millionaire rookies in particular contempt. Especially imperiled vets like Steve DeBerg, Elway's competition.

"I thought he could have helped more," Elway said.

"John came here with the idea that he wanted to be one of the guys, and I don't think anyone was going to let him be for a while, just because of the buildup," wide receiver Steve Watson said.

Added guard Keith Bishop: "John had to put up with a lot of crap in the locker room that no one will ever know about. People who were supposed to be working together were working against him."

Like all rookies, Elway also was a slow learner, especially in Reeves' complexly coded schemes. Former Oakland quarterback Kenny Stabler boasted he studied his playbook from the light of a juke box. Elway pulled near all-nighters, since he needed to know 90-100 plays on a typical Sunday — as well as innumerable formations, options and defenses.

A sample play: "Red right eagle rover opposite 5 power 49 EGO rover bootleg, left right, on one."

Though it sounded complex, Reeves' system was rudimentary in intent, at least to Elway, who was accustomed to sophisticated passing schemes.

"I called it 'The Edsel' system," Watson said. "It was a Neanderthal system that focused on keeping guys in to protect instead of attacking a defense. Instead of getting five guys in the routes, they get three guys, and so outlets were few and far between."

Broncos coach Mike Shanahan winces when reminded of Elway's early years.

"If John Elway had come out of his rookie year with the type of players and the system we have now, I think he'd have a number of Super Bowls under his belt," he said. "When I was with John for three Super Bowls (1986, '87, '89), I would come back at the end of the season and try to put tapes together and take them to clinics. I'd try to explain what we were doing on offense, but most of the plays were just John free-wheeling and making something happen when everything broke down."

Elway was at his free-wheeling best on a warm, wet August night in 1983.

Despite flashes of brilliance, Elway struggled to learn Reeves' offense. As the miscues increased, so did his anxiety. "I began worrying about success, about the outcome of things. I was worrying about every play. I became my own worst enemy."

The NFL refuses to call its pre-season games exhibitions, but Elway's debut was an exhibition in the classic sense. The Broncos met Seattle at Mile High Stadium, and the NFL met its purported savior.

Elway entered the game in the fourth quarter, to thunderous approval.

"My heart rate went from 130 above 180 to 200 over 150 when I went in," he said.

He handed off on the first play, completed a short pass on the second, then a couple more.

After his first NFL incompletion, Elway shifted into shotgun formation, took the center snap, scanned his options, then zapped a 38-yard bullet to Watson.

"When John first came in, the first thing he said to us in the huddle was this — he smiled real big and said — 'Guys don't let me down.'" Watson said. "There's a big play brewing every time he comes up to the line of scrimmage.

On the ninth play, Rick Upchurch was draped by two defenders as he crossed the middle of the field. But Elway found the only opening, and the Broncos had the ball on the 2. On the next play, Sammy Winder ran it in, as Elway signaled touchdown.

"He's electric," linebacker Tom Jackson said. "The man is just electric. I knew the fans were in for a treat when he ran onto the field. I knew it would happen."

During a rain-drenched 10-play scoring drive, Elway had completed five of six passes and set off a reaction that was extreme, even by Broncos standards.

"It's a bird, it's a plane .. it's John Elway" screamed a page-one *Rocky Mountain News* headline. In all, the *News* had 10 stories, five photos and a chart on the game. *The Post* had eight stories, five charts, one graph plus 14 photos, including two in color and one on the front page.

It was an unforgettable performance — unfortunately for Elway.

Elway had performed his personal brand of magical realism against rookies, free agents and third teamers, not the front-line players he'd see when the games counted. And that made his long fall even harder.

Rookie quarterbacks usually fail. Dallas' Troy Aikman had an 0-11 record as a starter and threw nearly twice as many interceptions as touchdowns. Randall Cunningham's quarterback rating (29.8 percent) and record as a starter (1-3) were galling. Terry Bradshaw became a human dart board for critics, many of whom were teammates.

"When things didn't go right, they just tapped a finger to their head and figured I was dumb. And I had nobody to defend me," Bradshaw said.

"I was totally unprepared for pro football."

But Elway had a bigger problem: He had been appointed the franchise's savior, and then gone out and proved he was worthy of that designation in his first pre-season game.

The pressure on Elway intensified when Reeves — in a move he later called fatal — made him the starter before a pre-season game at Minnesota.

The Vikings played football the old-fashioned way — brutally. Even their 'glamour' players were hard-core warriors, including quarterback Joe Kapp, who set the sullen tone in 1967 when he crossed the Canadian border to join the NFL.

"The first time we ever saw him ... he came up to the line of scrimmage and said, "(Expletive) you, Rams. I'm coming right at you," recalled former Los Angeles Rams Deacon Jones.

The Vikings blitzed Elway from start to end, which is standard procedure against rookies. When Elway wasn't on his back (he was sacked five times) he was about to be.

On the flight home, following a 34-3 loss in which he completed only 11 passes for 111 yards, Elway saw giant Vikings chasing him in his nightmares.

"I wish success could happen overnight," he said.

The Broncos opened the regular season on the road against the Pittsburgh Steelers.

"This guy is the best thing that has happened to this league in a long time," NBC analyst Bob Trumpy said before the opening kickoff at Three Rivers Stadium. "Elway not only has ability, he has the all-American good looks. With

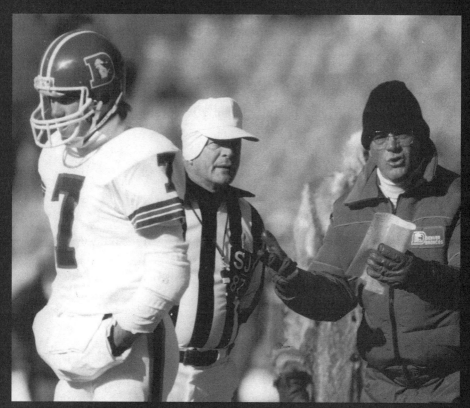

Elway and Reeves had many disputes over the years, often stemming from their differences over strategy. Elway, not surprisingly, wanted to employ a sophisticated passing scheme. Reeves insisted on a more conservative running oriented-approach.

all the bad publicity the NFL has had the past two years, Elway is just what the doctor ordered."

Elway soon needed a doctor. Like Minnesota, the Steelers pride themselves on brutal, intimidating play. On the first play, he looked across the line of scrimmage into the eyes of Steeler linebacker Jack "Fangs" Lambert, who led the league in meanness.

Five years before, after teammate Jack Ham had picked off a San Francisco 49ers pass, Lambert grabbed him by the shoulder pads and started violently shaking and spitting at him.

A weird macho rite of celebration?

Not quite.

Lambert was fuming because Ham had entered his "zone" to make a scene-stealing play.

San Francisco rookie Mike Shumann, the intended receiver, said, "I was making about 25 grand at the time and I remember thinking, 'I can make more money bartending. Do I really want to play in this league with those psychos?'"

The same thought occurred to Elway.

"I was standing right across the line from him," Elway recalls. "He had no teeth and he was slobbering all over, and I'm thinking, 'You can have your money back — just get me out of here. Let me go be an accountant.' I can't even tell you how bad I wanted out of there."

Archie Manning knows the sensation. As he prepared to make his first NFL start — against the Los Angeles Rams' Fearsome Foursome — he went into meltdown mode in New Orleans.

"They'd just installed turf in Tulane Stadium, and it must have been about 130 degrees on the field," said the Saints' quarterback.

In the Saints locker room, Manning almost passed out. A trainer told him to remove his uniform, then gave him something to drink. Manning gathered his resources, then managed to lead the Saints to victory.

Elway wasn't as fortunate.

He completed his first and only pass on the Broncos' fourth possession. He threw his first interception on the next play and was sacked for the first time a few minutes later.

Nothing went right. On third and three in the first quarter, Lambert decked Elway, who dropped the ball trying to save his head. Elway completed only one of eight passes for 14 yards, was sacked four times, and had to limp off the field and watch DeBerg lead the team to a 14-10 win.

The nightmare was only beginning.

The following week, by an irony of scheduling, the Broncos played in Baltimore, which was ripe for retribution.

"I'd like to put a helmet in John Elway's sternum," Baltimore linebacker Gary Padjen said.

Tight end Pat Beach asked Kush if he could play on the defense "for one series ... I want to get a clean shot at him."

"I want to see him killed," a female fan said.

"Don't hold back, guys," a sportscaster told the team.

On the day of the game, the *Baltimore Evening American* ran a cartoon featuring ways to honor No. 7: "A two-second highlight film of Elway's debut against the Steelers will be shown ... At game time, Elway will be appointed honorary captain and lose the coin flip, threatening to join the Yankees if his team doesn't receive first ... During special pre-game ceremonies Elway's number will be retired. Other parts of Elway will be retired in five-minute intervals thereafter."

Almost fittingly, it was 100 degrees, the hottest Sept. 11 in Baltimore history. Signs of unrest were everywhere: "Kill Elway ... Elway Sucks ... Union Memorial Hospital Awaits John 'Wimp' Elway ... Blow Away Elway ... Hope You Can Take the Heat."

"I'm fed up with all of this; I'll be glad to get it over," Elway mumbled.

"If (they) really go out with the intention of getting Elway, they'll find themselves in a lot of trouble," warned Broncos linebacker Tom Jackson.

Fans booed Elway when he came out for warm-ups, during warm-ups, and after warm-ups. "They even cheered when he missed a pass in warm-ups," DeBerg said.

When Elway returned to the field the booing resumed.

"I wasn't going out there alone, but I couldn't find anyone who wanted to walk with me," he joked.

The sheer volume of hate prevented Elway from being heard in the huddle, which increased the sense of disorder.

For example, Elway stepped slowly to the line of scrimmage on one play, oblivious to the fact that only two seconds remained on the 30-second clock. Tight end Ron Egloff had not even started in motion, but Reeves had.

Moments later flags were flying, whistles were blowing, and Reeves was still jumping up and down in rage.

On another play, as the 30-second clock wound down again, Elway decided to let it run all the way down. The Colts jumped offside, giving Denver a first down since it was fourth and two.

Sadly, that qualified as Elway's best play on a day when he completed nine of 21 passes for only 106 yards.

Reeves yanked him shortly afterward, which amounted to an act of mercy. DeBerg came in again, completing nine of 11 passes, including one for a touchdown, during a 17-10 victory.

On that long, ugly day, the Colts fumbled three times — yet the Broncos didn't once fall on the ball before it caromed out of bounds. Colts quarterback Mike Pagel, whom Irsay had mistakenly called Jim before the game, was sacked four times, intercepted three times, and converted one of 14 third downs. But a bad day got worse in the bitter aftermath, when Elway went his own unsweet way.

Fans threw garbage at him as he headed to the showers, and some vaulted down to the field, where they were handcuffed and arrested.

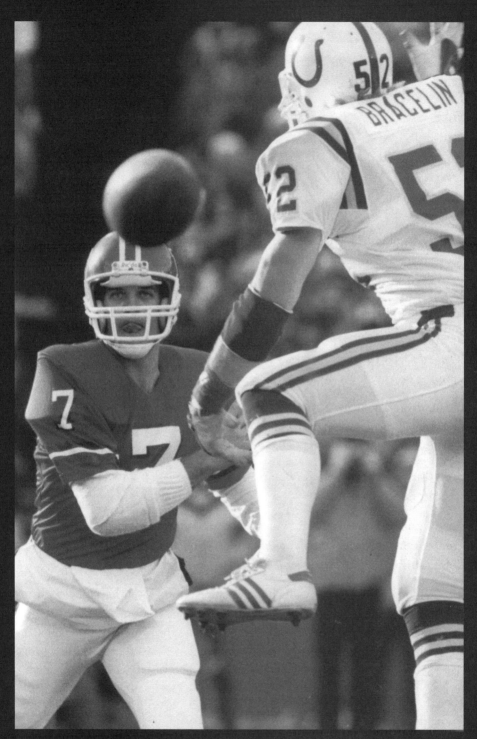

Elway is known as the Comeback King because of his classic game-saving drives. No. 1 came in his rookie season against the Baltimore Colts, who had humiliated him earlier in the season. The Broncos trailed 19-0 in the fourth quarter at Mile High Stadium. Elway threw three TD passes, the last a 26-yarder to Gerald Willhite with 44 seconds left in a 21-19 win.

"They seemed to enjoy seeing people hurt," linebacker Tom Jackson said.

"I doubt what happened to him has ever happened before," DeBerg said.

Several feet away, Reeves was being pressed to replace Elway with DeBerg.

"There's no way I'm going to leave him now," Reeves said. "I don't even think that's a reasonable thought."

Elway, who was 10-for-29 after two games, had little to say in the sauna-like locker room afterward.

"I'm bewildered," he said.

"It hasn't been much fun so far," Elway added. "But I've gone up against Pittsburgh and the big buildup of my first game and Baltimore, which loves me to death. Two of the toughest are out of the way."

But Elway's days as a starter were numbered. Elway had discovered he couldn't rely on natural talent — as he had all his life — to salvage a play. His offensive line was inconsistent, and he couldn't read defenses well. In fact, critics suggested Elway might lack the intelligence to decipher sophisticated defenses, a surprising allegation against a man who had earned a degree in economics from Stanford.

"That was the worst part — that I wasn't intelligent," he said. "That I was dumb and couldn't pick up the offense. That galled me the most."

The fact that Elway's intelligence had been questioned, much like Terry Bradshaw's a decade before, pushed Reeves to the limit of his patience, as well.

"There's nothing wrong with John Elway's intelligence," he said. "I think one thing which enters into it is that things came so naturally for all the great quarterbacks on their way to the pros. John was never in a situation where he had to study, dig and scrape to be good. This is his life now. Remember, he's young and it has taken him time to understand he must dedicate himself to learning."

The support for Elway among some teammates was inertial. Others wanted DeBerg to run the show. The conflict alone was disturbing to Elway, not to mention unprecedented.

"Whenever you've got one guy on the bench who some of the other players think should be starting, it doesn't make for a good situation," he said.

Added Reeves: "I think John wants so badly for the other players on the team to accept him. Steve DeBerg didn't come in and immediately gain the respect of everyone; he earned it. John gets so frustrated, he wants to gain their respect right now. When he does that, he'll get over one very big battle."

Just when it couldn't get worse for Elway, it did, especially on the road, where fans heaped scorn on the $5 million rebel.

"If I had it to do over," Elway said later, "I'd play where I was drafted. My attitude about it really made things hard for me. That's when the 'spoiled brat' image really began. I had the best of two worlds in football and baseball, and I was pushing to get my own way. If I had to do it over again, I'd do it differently."

The end came against Chicago, during a defeat that mercifully enabled Elway to temporarily escape from his own life. Reeves had tried to simplify the offense by reducing his options to five formations per game, compared to the 15 he gave DeBerg. He also had DeBerg signaling formation calls from the sidelines.

But the statistics told the story. The Bears won 31-14, and Elway had done nothing to even delay the defeat. He was four for 10 for 36 yards, when Reeves, quite appropriately, benched him.

A couple days later, Elway and a couple teammates headed to Wyoming to escape the media and fan firestorm. It was there that Elway realized what it meant to be the Broncos quarterback.

Elway had spent his teen years adjacent to Hollywood, where celebrity sightings are as mundane as freeways. Jack Nicholson? Paul Newman? Magic Johnson? Tommy Lasorda?

They come, they go; outside, the world still turns.

"We don't have motion picture or television or recording personalities," Saccomano added. "John Denver lives somewhere out in the mountains. Kurt Russell, Goldie Hawn, Hunter Thompson have homes in Aspen or Vail. But in Denver, what prominent figure would someone expect to see in a restaurant? I don't think anybody would get excited about seeing the president of Coors. No, it's going to be a sports figure."

Elway was the absolute pinnacle of Rocky Mountain celebrity-hood, which he finally realized on his descent.

"We're sitting there in Wyoming at this roadside restaurant, and this guy sitting next to us is saying I lost every game for us," Elway said. "Suddenly, I realized it was coming across to people on the outside that it was all my fault. I'm not saying it wasn't, but you couldn't blame everything on one guy, especially a rookie quarterback. It was hard not to resent some of what was happening. That's when I knew I'd never be afforded the one thing every other rookie is afforded — to be a rookie.

"Ninety-five percent of the fans are just great, but it's the five percent which make you bitter. When I go out I'm supposed to be the perfect person, but I want to be like their next-door neighbor rather than John Elway. I'm just like any other person. I'm no different from anyone else."

"If I'm a celebrity, it's not in the way I'd like it to be. I haven't proven anything to anybody. If a kid comes up to me and asks for an autograph, I want to be able to feel good about writing my name down on that piece of paper. I just don't feel I've proven anything. If you sign your name and become a celebrity, you'd better have proven it."

Actually, Elway found peace from the mollifying distance of the sideline, where he realized his troubles extended beyond technical matters.

"There was so much hype early that I was the savior of the Denver Broncos," he said. "It bothered me. Then the frustration of failing worked against me. The worse things went, the more bad things were said, and the harder I tried. I put too much pressure on myself.

"I began worrying about success, about the outcome of things. I was worrying about every play. I became my own worst enemy.

"By the Chicago game I was so confused my mind was going 100 miles a minute, and as soon as you start thinking like that you don't react. I worried about remembering the plays. I worried about calling the formations and getting the play without a delay-of-game penalty. I couldn't even think about the defense.

At the start of his rookie season, Elway found himself in the middle of a media storm. By season's end, he was just another guy in the locker room.

"It's a terrible feeling to drop back and not know what's going on in front of you ... The Chicago game was the bottom. I dug myself a hole, and I couldn't get out of it."

In effect, Reeves gave Elway the month off, who didn't see any action against Houston, Cincinnati, San Diego and Kansas City. Instead, while DeBerg ran the show, he had time to unwind and then re-acquaint himself with the offense. Hadl prevented Elway from becoming complacent, a common fate for backup quarterbacks. Elway drove himself, as well, attending extra film sessions.

When DeBerg injured his shoulder, Elway returned in Week 10 and started five games, including one against San Diego he wished he hadn't.

Shortly before intermission, during a time-out, he and Reeves selected a play, talked it over, and then Elway forgot to put the receiver in proper position when he set the formation. It went for an interception, triggering a sideline shouting match with Reeves.

"He got mad. I got mad. I don't know. When you're struggling, you don't want to hear how bad you're doing," Elway said.

The argument sent Elway into a second-half tailspin that culminated when he lined up behind guard Tom Glassic instead of center.

"He had his hands under me, and I was trying to kick his foot," Glassic said. "Billy (Bryan) and I were yelling, 'Wrong guy, wrong guy.' It was disastrous, but you have to laugh about it or you'd cry."

After another dislocated day — and defeat — the jet that was supposed to take the Broncos home couldn't land in San Diego because of a heavy fog. Elway considered it a symbol of sorts — a punitive one.

"This is always what I've wanted to do — stay in San Diego, after I've got my butt kicked,"

A couple days later, Reeves and Elway met in private.

"I told him we're bad for each other," Reeves said. "We're both impatient. We made a pact after that game. I told him I'd remind him to be patient if he'd remind me. With so much talent in one individual, I expected him to go out and perform miracles. It was unfair on my part. I now realize that I didn't know how much was involved in starting a rookie quarterback.

"I shouldn't have made him the starter. I had Steve DeBerg and after five pre-season games, they were about even. John was young, with all the tools, so I went with him. It was a big mistake. Nobody plays the same in pre-season as they do in the regular season. Teams threw everything at him, and I couldn't help him.

"The biggest mistake was in thinking we could be basic, that we could move the football by being basic. There were two reasons that didn't work: The first was that we weren't talented enough to be basic. We couldn't say 'Look out, here we come.'

"The second, and probably the most important, is that I can't coach a basic offense."

But on Dec. 4 Elway guided the Broncos to a 27-6 win over Cleveland. Seven days later, during a game against the Colts, the team that had all but set a bounty on his head 12 weeks before, Elway provided a preview of coming attractions.

For three quarters, nothing went right for either him or the team, which was quite all right with Irsay, who felt redemption was near. Elway connected with John Sawyer for a first down, and then Sawyer fumbled. He hit Steve Watson for a long gainer, and then a couple plays later Elway fumbled at the goal line.

In the first half Elway had completed only seven of 14 passes for 98 yards.

"We had him rattled with our blitzes," cornerback Tate Randle said.

On and on it went. Entering the final quarter, the Broncos trailed 19-0. That's when Comeback No. 1 of Elway's NFL career began.

In 10 minutes, Elway struck back — against everything. On third and 10 on Baltimore's 21, he threw a touchdown pass to Clint Sampson. On third and four on the Baltimore 26, Elway threw a touchdown pass to Jesse Myles.

With three minutes left, the Broncos had the ball at their 25. The Colts started blitzing en masse, but Elway moved the Broncos to the 26-yard line with 52 seconds left. On fourth down, with the game on the line, Elway connected with Gerald Willhite for the winning touchdown. The Broncos' 21-19 win secured a playoff berth.

"Today kind of epitomized what this team is all about," Elway said. "We were down 19-0, with a chance to get in the playoffs, and everybody hung together and fought back. I knew we had plenty of time. I'm a competitor.

"After all those people talked about how we (Stanford) never played in a bowl game, it's nice to make the playoffs in my first year."

Elway didn't feel the same two weeks later.

On Dec. 22, Elway was benched — for the second time. After Reeves learned that DeBerg was in shape to play in an AFC Divisional playoff game against Seattle, Reeves opted for the vet.

"Coach Reeves wanted me to come in for a talk," Elway said. "Keith Uecker and I drove in together and we were talking. 'What do you think Coach Reeves wants to talk about?' The fourth thing on our list was the possibility of Steve DeBerg coming back as the starting quarterback. I thought that possibility was a distant one because I didn't think he would be ready to play.

"I've hit the all-time lows and the all-time highs this season. I could have gone in the bucket after this, but no way. The whole year has been a test for me, and this is just part of it.

"It's been an interesting year, though, hasn't it? If anybody could talk about a rookie season, I guess I could."

After a 31-7 playoff drubbing by Seattle, Elway chatted with a few reporters — the rest had more pressing business — collected his gear and exited a nightmare.

The final stark stats said it all: 259 passing attempts, 123 completions, .475 completion percentage, 1,663 yards, seven touchdowns, 14 interceptions.

His quarterback rating of 54.9 was the worst in the AFC.

Meanwhile, Dan Marino led the AFC in passing, the first man to do so since the 1970 merger, and was a Pro Bowl starter.

Only months before, Elway was everybody's ultimate No. 1 draft pick, and Marino an afterthought. The paradox was haunting.

"He was in a totally different situation than I was," Elway said. "He walks onto a team that was in the Super Bowl the year before, and he's got talent. The key thing they were missing was a quarterback.

"I still stand by my saying, that I wouldn't trade anything I've got for what he's got."

The next year Marino would unleash the most devastating passing attack ever seen. Elway would try merely to survive.

Not surprisingly, he headed home to California at season's end. Elway played some golf, married his fiancee, took in some Stanford baseball games, drank some beers, and ultimately tried to recover from the most harrowing year of his 23-year-old life.

"I remember after we were married, John helped his father at Stanford, working with players," Janet Elway said. "He loved it. At one point, he talked to me about forgetting pro football and becoming an assistant for his father. I don't think deep down he was serious. But I know he thought about it."

No matter what he did, Elway was hot copy at his first training camp. Nearly 30 media members lived in an adjacent dorm in Greeley to chronicle his development. Everyone wanted to know how he did in training camp. He was always eager to outrun the press, his mode of escape, in this instance, being a scooter.

It didn't take long for Elway to regain his bravado following his shaky rookie season. As he drove his team to comeback victories over New England, and San Diego (twice) he became the team's undisputed leader, as well as its spokesman. Here he asks fans for silence.

Chapter 4 —
The Comeback Kid

FOR A BRITTLE MOMENT IN NOVEMBER, 1996, AT THE
Oakland Coliseum, all the action had been knocked out of John Elway.

The Broncos' brawny quarterback is built to last, but as he limped off the field
during the fourth quarter of a Monday night game against the reviled Raiders,
clutching a hamstring, even he seemed too dented and depleted to save another
day.

But Elway is always armed for the unexpected, especially with danger brewing.

By ancient reflex, Elway stepped back into play, reached back, cocked the trigger,
and then fired a 49-yard scoring strike to Rod Smith.

It stunned Oakland and gave the Broncos a 22-21 victory, and their 36-year-old
quarterback his 40th fourth-quarter comeback.

At 6-foot-2, 225-pounds, Elway is the prototype of the modern quarterback. His
arms, legs, chest and overall strength are the raw materials of greatness. But
Elway's greatest strength lies in never considering retreat.

Entering his 15th season, Elway had led the Broncos to 41 game-saving drives in
the final quarter. He's done it 20 times with under three minutes remaining, 10
times with under two minutes, and 12 with under one minute.

He'd done it against AFC teams and NFC teams, at home and on the road, with
nothing and everything on the line, in hellish heat and polar cold. In fact,
Elway's had to duplicate himself as the Broncos' savior for months of Sundays
for years on end.

But before he saved the franchise, Elway had to save himself.

After his rookie meltdown, Elway wasn't guaranteed success. Plenty of whiz kids have seen their wonderful futures whiz right on by. Over six decades, only two Heisman Trophy-winning quarterbacks have made it big in the NFL: Roger Staubach and Jim Plunkett. The rest — with the possible exception of Vinny Testaverde, who turned in the best season of his career with the Baltimore Ravens in 1966 — just wandered off football's radar screens, along with dozens of other All-Americans and passing prodigies.

Joe Montana was only a third-round pick, which underscores the difficulty of measuring a quarterback's game. In fact, many of the crucial qualities are immeasurable: the will to win, the ability to cope with failure and adversity, the drive to succeed at all costs.

But everyone who knew Elway knew he was no passing star. He was different.

It was different at Elway's second training camp. First, rival Steve DeBerg was gone, traded to Tampa Bay to become Steve Young's backup. Second, Mike Shanahan had arrived, with a blueprint for Elway's future.

It's no coincidence that under Shanahan, Elway won three AFC championships, played in three Super Bowls and compiled all but 13 of his 41 comeback victories; and that without Shanahan a gate shut on Elway's dreams.

In 1984, Shanahan was Denver's receivers coach; in 1985 offensive coordinator. In reality he was Elway's guru. He summoned and then smoothed all his skills, just as Bill Walsh did with Joe Montana and Norv Turner would later do with Troy Aikman.

"Without question it's the most important relationship on a team," Walsh told *Sports Illustrated* in 1995. "That's because the quarterback is under such tremendous stress. The entire defensive team is after him, and consciously or unconsciously it wants to knock him out of the game. He's being threatened, and if he doesn't get full support around him or doesn't have confidence in the person calling plays, he's going to crumble."

At first glance, Elway and Shanahan had little in common. Elway is all fire and passion, brimming with big-fisted dexterity and easy-going banter. Shanahan is cerebral, icy cool and happiest when immersed in the technical arcana of plotting the perfect play or mastering the esoteric details of the salary cap.

But from the first practice, Shanahan's practiced eye and Elway's unbounded ambition made them a matchless pair.

"When I first came in here and started coaching John, I was 31, and John was really just getting started. He struggled a bit in the first year, so when I came in, I put him on a weight-training program and even lifted with him," Shanahan said. "We developed a close relationship, and out of that grows friendship."

Shanahan and Elway played golf, drank beers, plotted strategy, analyzed opponents, traded war stories and, if none of Denver's wide receivers could be summoned to the practice field in the off-season, Shanahan would lace up his cleats and play catch with the $5 million quarterback at a nearby park.

"There's a bond there, a trust there, there's a belief in one another," Shanahan said. "I think that really helps a coach when a player knows you care about him. You've been through the wars together. He knows how you react under pressure. He knows that when the going gets tough, you're going to be there for him. You're not going to turn your back, and I think those are special bonds."

Added Elway: "We get along well, and maybe it's because we're a lot alike. Any time we do something we're always competing to beat the other guy. That's one of the top attractions with him."

Although Dan Reeves later fired Shanahan, claiming he and Elway scripted plays behind his back, Reeves is upfront about Shanahan's role in Elway's rise.

"John had his best years when Mike was coaching him," Reeves said. "Mike knew how to get the most out of him. So there was just a respect there between the two guys that's obviously still there. When John was at a critical moment in his career, along came Mike at the right time."

Step One was pumping up Elway's strength.

"I got hurt a couple times my first years, so I put on 10 or 15 pounds of padding," Elway said. "It was a cushion of muscle. It really helped. I realized how important my mobility is to me. I knew I had to improve the strength in my legs."

It helped Elway mentally as well.

"After that first year when I was a big bust, I just wanted to prove people wrong. If you believe you're stronger, that's a big step."

Elway's 1984 stats were mundane: 2,598 yards, 18 touchdowns. In 1985, he set club single-season records for attempts (605), completions (327) and passing yards (3,891).

By 1986, he earned his first Pro Bowl berth and compiled a career-high 79 percent quarterback rating. But perhaps the best measure of Elway's comeback were his comebacks.

"Nobody plays Denver without worrying if that could be the game Elway explodes," Cincinnati Bengals coach Sam Wyche said. "John's a time bomb waiting to go off."

In 1984, Elway led the Broncos on an eight-play, 78-yard drive that set up a 26-19 win over New England. Against San Diego he led the Broncos on a 10-play, 77-yard drive that ended in a 16-13 victory when Sammy Winder scored on a 1-yard run with 38 seconds left. Elway guided the Broncos to another 16-13 win over San Diego with a 12-play, 40-yard drive that set up Rich Karlis' game-winning field goal with 2:08 left.

In 1985, Elway produced come-from-behind wins over Atlanta, San Francisco, San Diego, Pittsburgh, Kansas City and Seattle.

With his John Wayne swagger, guns' a blazin' bravado and calm authority, Elway was becoming a gunslinger incarnate.

"A slinger is a guy who makes throws other guys won't even attempt," Elway says. "At times, you make bad decisions. People wonder why you even made the throw. On the other hand, you make the big play the other guy can't even try."

Great gunslingers are an enduring, endearing part of NFL lore. It all started with slingin' Sammy Baugh, who introduced the passing game to the NFL in the '30s, along with the brimming spirit and hunger for glory that possessed dashing, darting Bobby Layne in the '50s and early '60s, Roger Staubach in the '70s, and Elway in the '80s and '90s.

Elway possessed all the quirks and merits of classic slingers. Great arm. Cunning mobility and expansive field vision. Great improvisational skills. And battle nerves.

"I used to run around the backyard, imagining I was Roger Staubach," he said.

Nothing excites Elway more than a Big Game. He established himself as a bonafide NFL star when he lead the Broncos to a 23-20 victory over Cleveland in the 1986 AFC Championship Game with The Drive. The Broncos moved 98 yards in 15 plays to send the game into overtime, and Elway into a state of joy.

Staubach was an ideal role model. When the heat was on, he broke down a defense using all his assets — arms, legs, eyes, mind.

So does Elway.

No need to tell Marty Schottenheimer, who coached Cleveland and Kansas City to great success except against Denver's Master of Disaster.

In 1989, Kansas City and Denver were knotted 13-13 as time wound down. Elway marched Denver 71 yards in 10 plays to set up David Treadwell's 26-yard field goal with one second left. The next year, with the Chiefs ahead 23-21, Elway connected with Vance Johnson on a 49-yarder on fourth-and-10. Four plays later, Treadwell kicked a 22-yard field goal as time expired.

In 1991, Denver was tied with the Chiefs 16-16 with 5:40 left at Mile High Stadium. The Broncos had scored just three points in the second half, thanks to the Chiefs' pass rush, which chased Elway with determined efficiency.

After linebacker Derrick Thomas and defensive end Bill Maas sacked him once more, the Broncos faced third and 17 at their own 13.

But in situations like these, defending against Elway is like picking up a dangerous wire.

This time, Elway bootlegged to his right, stopped, set his feet, turned his shoulders, and threw it to the opposite sideline to Mark Jackson as he raced to the left sideline. The ball traveled 61 yards on the fly and 71 in all.

"It took off like a driver," center Keith Kartz later said of the pass.

Four plays later, Treadwell kicked a game-winning 27-yarder.

"The guy's (Elway) been as good a competitor as there's ever been in this business and that's why he makes the plays," Schottenheimer said. "He is determined to find a way to get it done."

In 1992, the Broncos trailed Kansas City 19-6 with under four minutes left to play at Mile High Stadium. Fans were streaming out the exits, despite a plea from play-by-play announcer Larry Zimmer.

"For you on portable radios, you're making a mistake; this game is never over,"

Zimmer said.

Soon Elway fired a scoring pass to Mark Jackson.

"There were as many people pouring back in as there were pouring out," Zimmer recalled for NFL Films, which put out a video on Elway's comebacks.

The defense stopped the Chiefs on three plays, and with under two minutes left, they punted.

"Men, I'll tell you what. This is our opportunity to get it done right now with the defense — the best in the league," Schottenheimer told his defense.

Marshall fumbled the punt, near midfield, but picked the ball up and ran it into KC territory. Elway then threw a scoring strike to Vance Johnson, which put another stake into the heart of the Chiefs. As he ran off the field, his nerves jangling, the air was weighted with Elway's magic.

"One of the strengths is my competitiveness," he said. "I wouldn't trade that for anything — the will to win and never give up. I always want to win, no matter what.

"We had a lot of comebacks in high school. It got started there. We had some comebacks at Stanford. So when it came to Denver, and we got in those type of situations, I knew we could come through."

Former Kansas City quarterback Len Dawson, who led the Chiefs to a victory in Super Bowl IV, compared Elway to another great escape artist. "He's like Larry Bird: 'Give me the ball, I'll take the shot with the game on the line.' A lot of guys may say that, but he believes it. The simple question: 'Can I win it?' The simple answer: 'Yes'. And he transfers that to the team."

In a 1991 AFC divisional playoff game against Houston, the Oilers' Greg Montgomery punted to the Denver 2-yard line. With 2:07 and no time-outs remaining, Elway found himself in the same predicament as The Drive, his greatest drive of all, which lifted the Broncos to the 1986 AFC Championship game victory over Schottenheimer's Cleveland Browns.

"I remember running on to the field saying, 'Well, we're going to see if that first one was a fluke or not,'" Elway said.

Elway has always prided himself on his ability to see the big picture. His analytical skills were evident early, says Jack Elway, who, as a coach, trained him to look beyond his own position and to understand the other positions and how they're all linked together. Broncos fans began to realize that when Elway surveyed the field, his mind was already on the next play and the one after that.

On first down, Elway dropped back into the shotgun, and into the end zone. Then he gunned a pass to Michael Young for a 22-yard gain. Three plays later, Elway faced fourth-and-six at the 28. Elway dropped back, then scrambled left upfield and ran out of bounds just beyond the first-down marker.

"I remember feeling the pressure from the back side, so when I stepped up the first thing I saw was the first-down marker," he said. "I knew I could get the first down and stop the clock."

Three straight incompletions left Elway facing fourth and 10 near his 35. Only 59 seconds remained.

"They got a good pass rush from the back side, and I was able to step up through that and get outside," Elway said. "It was the same defense as last time. Only this time the cornerback came up to stop me from running. I saw Vance Johnson over the top."

Elway threw a wobbly ball that Johnson caught, and then sprinted down the left sideline to Houston's 21 for a 44-yard gain.

"That may be one of the worst passes I've ever thrown, but I've never had a guy that open in that situation where I just handed him the ball, so it wobbled a lot but fortunately it got there," he said.

Two plays later, Treadwell kicked a 28-yard field goal for a 26-24 Denver win.

In 1992, Houston scored a go-ahead touchdown with 1:56 left in a regular-season game at Mile High Stadium.

The Broncos regained possession on their own 20, trailing 21-20. On first down, Elway averted a sack, started to run upfield, then threw a 39-yard strike to Mark Jackson.

The Oilers, ranked among the AFC's best, threw everything at Elway on the next two plays, rushing six players en masse. The first time, Elway and Vance Johnson connected for a 20-yard gain. The second time Elway slipped the ball to Reggie Rivers, who raced untouched for the winning score.

Three plays, 80 yards, 22 seconds.

"It's so redundant," Houston defensive end Sean Jones said after the 27-21 loss.

"All of this is so redundant. I'll just say this: If you're playing the best 3-and-2 hitter in baseball, you don't run the count to 3-and-1 and give him two chances to beat you. If you're playing the best power-play team in hockey, you don't let it have a man advantage at a crucial time.

"If you know that Michael Jordan's got the best baseline jumper in basketball, you don't let him get the ball on the baseline late in the game. Same thing here. You don't give John Elway the ball with a chance to beat you with two minutes to go."

Sometimes it gets downright absurd. As time ran out in the Metrodome in 1996, Elway threw to Shannon Sharpe in the Minnesota Vikings end zone. The ball was deflected three times by two Minnesota defenders — straight into the hands of Ed McCaffrey, who tumbled into the end zone for the winning score.

It was Comeback No. 41 for No. 7.

"During the game, he has one voice. Then when the game is on the line, he has a different voice. It gets slower, calmer. You know something magical will happen," Sharpe said.

Added ex-Broncos receiver Steve Watson: "I don't think there's ever been anybody better at running the two-minute drill. You have guys like Montana, dropback passers who benefited from a particular system. But we were stuck with our system and John still did it."

Elway saved the Broncos — and a place for himself in NFL lore — in 1986.

Ohio is sacred ground to football's fundamentalists. It's the home of The Pro Football Hall of Fame; Woody Hayes' great Ohio State teams; legendary Massilon High, and for six decades, Cleveland Stadium, where Paul Brown, Otto Graham, Jim Brown, Lou Groza and other immortals of football romped until the Browns deserted it for Baltimore in 1995.

Before Art Modell moved the team to Baltimore, the official Browns Backers had 63,000 members and close to 200 chapters in the U.S., Japan, Great Britain and Australia.

The true believers sat in the Dawg Pound, where they earned the enmity of visiting players by wearing rubber basset-hound masks, throwing bones and howling in delight at their despair.

"They were dangerous to all," former Cleveland defensive tackle Bob Golic said. "One time I asked one of 'em, 'Who are you aiming for with those bones? He said. 'Anyone.' I said, 'Us too?' and he said, 'Sure.' There were several times I thought we were going to have to play half-court games."

Eventually the Browns banned dog bones and dog biscuits from the Dawg Pound, but not large foam-rubber replicas of bones. "Why is the guy allowed to have his three-foot dog bone and I'm not allowed to have my little biscuits?" one Dawg Pound member asked.

The fact grown men and women asked such questions explains the anxiety the Broncos felt as they entered Cleveland Stadium to play for a berth in the Super Bowl.

The Broncos weren't given much of a chance to win. Elway was hobbled by a sore ankle, and the Browns and quarterback Bernie Kosar were on a mighty roll.

With arctic winds blowing in off Lake Erie, and the sky gray and leaden, the elements seemed to favor Cleveland, as well.

Herman Fontenot scored on a 6-yard TD reception in the first quarter to open the scoring. In the second quarter, Gerald Willhite scored on a fourth-down plunge to lift the Broncos to a 10-7 lead. In the fourth quarter, with the score tied 13-13, Cleveland wide receiver Brian Brennan slipped by Denver safety Dennis Smith and caught a third-down, 48-yard TD heave from Kosar. Cleveland led 20-13.

The Broncos botched the ensuing kickoff, and when Ken Bell finally fell on the ball, the Broncos had the ball on their 2-yard line.

"There wasn't much going our way," Tom Jackson said.

As they gathered on the goal line, waiting out a TV time-out, the Broncos looked like doomed zombies.

Finally lineman Keith Bishop broke the eerie spell. "We've got 'em right where we want 'em," he cracked.

"We had enough characters in that huddle between Keith Bishop and Billy

Many veterans treated Elway with icy contempt when he first arrived in Denver. Wide receiver Steve Watson, however, was quick to befriend the quarterback, and they developed a rapport both on and off the field. The Elway-Watson connection rose to the moment on The Drive, and then, in overtime, when they combined for a 28-yard gain that set up Rich Karlis' winning field goal.

Bryan and Paul Howard to actually be confident," Watson said. "You had a lot of overachievers on that team. I don't know if we had the overall talent of the teams of today, but I don't think there was ever a bunch that played better as a team.

"But it all came down to John. It was such a hostile, hostile atmosphere. And it had been a bloodbath all day long. They beat the tar out of me all day. There were so many little battles going on all throughout the course of the day. But it was amazing. John had his rhythm. And he was so confident.

"I truly will always remember the look on John's face. It was a look of absolute confidence. There was this grin, like, 'We've got it.'"

The drive got off to a good start when Elway hit Sammy Winder on a 5-yard swing pass. "They probably were thinking we'd try to run it to get it from the 2," Shanahan said. "So we run the trap and it looks like a run, we fake the run and hit the halfback in the flat."

On second down, Elway handed off to Sammy Winder, who gained three more yards.

The Broncos, who had been one for 12 on third downs, faced a dilemma. Do they go for it on fourth down if they don't make it on third? Winder ran up the middle to the 12. The officials called for a measurement. First down, Broncos.

On the next play, Elway handed off once more to Winder, who gained three yards. But with their goal line in the far-off distance, the Broncos were running out of time and, it appeared, energy.

"The key thing to realize is that if you don't think you can get the job done, the rest of the team starts wondering," Elway said. "You gotta keep a positive attitude. If you think you can get it done, you figure out a way how to get it done."

Elway scrambled 11 yards despite a wobbly right ankle on the next play, then dived for the first down.

"I knew I could get a first down. I got as far as I could, and then went down," he said.

The clock wound down below 3:00, but the Broncos had two time-outs remaining.

The Browns were getting jittery.

"The hard part is that no matter how confident you are about yourself, you've got a big problem because of Elway," Golic said. "There's no question how he's going to respond because he's proved time after time how good he is. So you're saying, 'Damn, we got to do our very best, but even if we do, it might not even make a difference because Elway is so good.'"

On the next play, Elway threw a 22-yard pass to Steve Sewell, moving the ball to Denver's 48. On the next play he drilled a 12-yard pass to Steve Watson at the Browns' 40.

Following the two-minute warning, Elway missed Johnson on a pass. On second down, Browns tackle Dave Puzzuoli grabbed Elway's right leg and sacked him for an 8-yard loss.

In the huddle, Elway clutched his face-mask, licked his fingers, implored his teammates to seize the moment. Then the Broncos lined up in the shotgun facing 3rd and 18.

Elway, flanked by Willhite on his right, and Watson on his left, gave a foot signal to send Watson in formation. But center Billy Bryan thought the signal was for him to snap the ball, which he did promptly. The ball deflected off Watson's buttocks toward Elway, who stooped low to catch the snap.

Gathering himself, Elway hit Mark Jackson for a 20-yard gain. No sweat.

"The thing that was amazing to me was that if it was third and 18, he picked up 19. Or if it was third and 12, he picked up 13," Golic said. "Nothing could go wrong with him. He did exactly what he needed to do. Everything was going his way. "

A hush fell over Cleveland Stadium.

"You gotta get lucky," Elway said. "There was no question we got lucky in this situation because the crowd was so loud that we were in silent cadence, and I had motion with it and I was trying to time the motion with the silent count and we were just a little bit early with the snap and it hit Steve Watson and it barely got back, and I was fortunate to get it back. (But) I had great time — that's what you gotta have in that situation, and I was able to get Mark the ball."

The Browns, who were on the verge of a Super Bowl berth only minutes before, were leaking fear.

"I don't think it was resignation as much as disbelief," Golic said.

Exploiting the fact Cleveland was in a three-man rush, Elway flipped a little screen pass to Sewell, who ran for 14 yards but not out of bounds as the clock wound down to 1:07.

On first-and-10 at the 14, the Broncos let the clock run down instead of calling a time-out. Elway tossed a pass to the sideline that Watson caught — out of bounds with 1:05 left.

On second down, Elway shook off one defender, then scrambled toward the first-down marker on the right sideline. Switching into baseball mode, he slid into the mud on the 5-yard line. On the drive's 15th play, with 42 seconds left, Elway spotted Jackson in the end zone. Then, like a pitcher throwing a fastball, he wound up and fired the most important touchdown pass of his career.

"I can remember saying to myself, 'Get this ball to him as fast as you can get it to him.' I don't remember ever throwing the ball as hard as I threw that ball. It was a low heater because if Mark didn't get it, no one was going to get it."

After Rich Karlis' extra-point kick, the Broncos could smell victory on the arctic wind. The Browns were already blown away.

"The field was littered with dog bones," Karlis said. "Missing the kick never crossed my mind."

In overtime, Elway hit Orson Mobley for a 22-yard gain, and connected with Watson for a 28-yarder. Four plays later, Rich Karlis kicked a 33-yard field goal to lift Denver to a 23-20 win, and a Super Bowl berth.

For a few frozen moments, Browns fans were brittle enough to shatter. Then they were stumbling mutely out of Cleveland Stadium, their worst fears realized. Meanwhile, Elway ran off the field in his earth-smeared jersey, in league, finally, with Johnny Unitas, Terry Bradshaw, Roger Staubach, Joe Montana, Dan Marino ....

"Being a leader, that is, having total control of your team, is above all the one asset a quarterback must have," Vince Lombardi had said a generation before. "A coach would like a skilled play-caller, a slick ball-handler and an accurate passer, but the one thing that is a must is having a person who can control any situation he is presented with. That requires a player with confidence, a forceful personality, and the ability to make his teammates believe in him as much as he does in himself.

"If you look at the great quarterbacks through the years — Graham, Layne, Unitas, Starr — they have had all that in common. In the final minutes of a close game, they could take control of their own team, which usually means taking control of — and winning — the game."

John Elway would have plenty of other dial-a-prayer victories and career-bending games in the years ahead. But none would compare with "The Drive."

"That was my coming-out party," he said. "That put me on the map. After being a bust in my rookie year, I'd come back."

Added Shanahan: "Elway is easily the most dangerous quarterback in the NFL. He can beat you in so many ways. He can kill you with one deep pass. He can get you by running or scrambling for a long gain after you think you've got him for a loss. And he can beat you with a ball-possession offense that takes advantage of his own running, short passing and leadership, as well as the abilities of his running backs. All of Elway's skills were put together in that last drive he engineered against Cleveland to win the 1986 AFC title game."

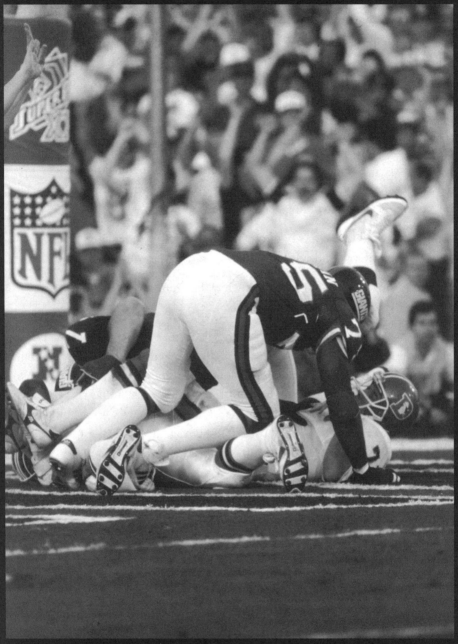

Elway quickly found his rhythm in his first Super Bowl, guiding the Broncos into scoring position on four of their first five possessions. Elway ran for a 4-yard score on the second possession, lifting the Broncos to a 10-7 lead. But after failing to score after gaining a first down on the Giants 1, the Broncos sagged. When George Martin dumped Elway for a safety, the Giants cut Denver's lead to 10-9 and set the tone for the rest of the game.

Chapter 5 — The Super Bowl Mess

AT HIS FIRST SUPER BOWL, JOHN ELWAY'S DREAMS WERE hardening into reality with each passing moment. Like a man dealing himself into history, he moved the Broncos into scoring position on four of their first five possessions at the Rose Bowl. So when they failed to score from the New York Giants' 1, on four plays, Elway regarded it as only a momentary setback.

Actually, it was the rubble preceding an avalanche.

The Broncos soon were buried under the weight of their own entangling mistakes and Phil Simms' passing brilliance. When the Giants rallied for a 39-20 victory in Super Bowl XXI, Elway was stunned, even shaken. When the Washington Redskins beat the Broncos 42-10 at the next Super Bowl, he was shamed. But when the San Francisco 49ers humiliated the Broncos 55-10 in XXIV, Elway hit bottom and went on, convinced only the ashes of his former glory remained.

For a quarterback attuned to the rhythm of the game's history, what could be worse than to lose three Super Bowls by a combined 96 points; to throw six interceptions and only two touchdowns; in front of an audience of 150 million Americans and 800 million worldwide, not to mention 3,000 media members from 180 countries — each time?

Elway had run out of answers. As he and his wife, Janet, strolled hand-in-hand in the Superdome, an hour or so after the 55-10 loss to San Francisco, John, pallid and weary, turned to pressing reporters and said, "Can't you guys let a guy sulk in peace?"

That might have been Elway's worst call of the day. There's no peace after the worst Super Bowl defeat in the history of Roman numerals, much less relief.

"Losing the Super Bowl is the ultimate humiliation," said a three-time loser, ex-Vikings quarterback Fran Tarkenton. "There is no consolation of any kind. People ridicule you and abuse you. They look much more kindly on teams that don't get there than a team that gets there and loses."

That's not an understatement. In the Super Bowl, a quarterback either carves his legacy, or digs his grave, in which case he's buried alive.

Joe Namath's career statistics are underwhelming, but he became an American icon by predicting and then delivering a victory over the Baltimore Colts in Super Bowl III. Richard Nixon even placed him on his enemies' list.

Terry Bradshaw ranked among the nation's most mocked athletes for years. Before Super Bowl XIII, Dallas Cowboys linebacker Hollywood Henderson said that Bradshaw was "so dumb he couldn't spell cat if you spotted him the c and a."

But Bradshaw retaliated by winning four Super Bowls, and now his name spells graceful champion. Joe Montana, a mediocre college quarterback, became Joe Montana via the Super Bowl. Roger Staubach, a forgotten college quarterback, will never be forgotten in NFL lore, not as long as his Super Bowl triumphs are recounted.

But Fran Tarkenton? John Elway? Jim Kelly? Dan Marino?

They're 0-3, 0-3, 0-4 and 0-1, respectively in the Super Bowl, for a combined 0-11 record. The Class of 1983's Elway, Kelly and Marino have combined for 18 Pro Bowl appearances, 16 division titles and eight conference championships, not to mention enough passing records to put them past belief. But they're 0-8 in the Big One.

Should that diminish their legacies? "Damn right", says Bradshaw.

"You feel a certain pity or sorrow for guys who don't play on great teams," he said. "There are a lot of great quarterbacks in the league who can put up a lot of stats. But the bottom line is that when you get in big games, you win those suckers. You've got to win championships because that's what it's all about.

"When you're all done, they say, 'Look bub, I know you threw for 100,000 yards and 500 touchdowns, but how many rings do you have?'"

Elway rushed for a team-high 27 yards in Super Bowl XXI, but often he was running for his life. Gerald Willhite gained just 19 yards on 4 carries. In all, the Broncos rushed 19 times for a paltry 52 yards, and an average of 2.7 yards per carry.

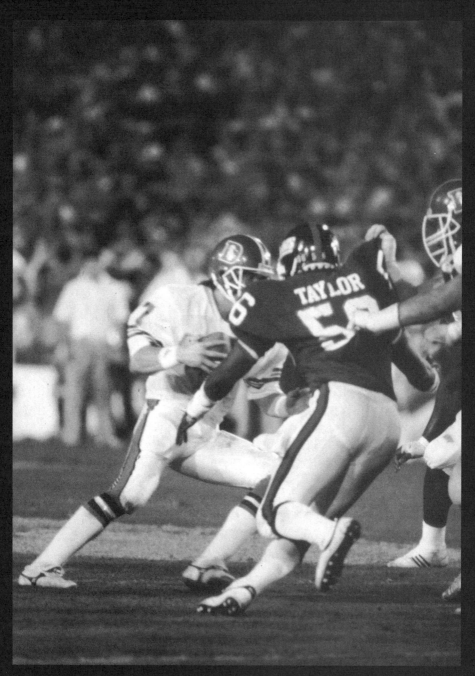

Lawrence Taylor, the Giants' legendary linebacker, tormented Elway and the Broncos. On first-and-goal from the Giants 1, Elway kept the ball, rolling to his right before aiming for the end zone. But Taylor stopped him in his tracks, then dumped him for a 1-yard loss. Three plays later, Rich Karlis blew a 23-yard field goal.

Jeff Hostetler, who guided the New York Giants to a 20-19 win over Buffalo in Super Bowl XXV, has a post-modern view of the Ultimate Game, as well.

"There is no reason to get there if you don't win," he said.

"I will not feel good about myself until I win one," Elway said.

The Super Bowl didn't always bend reason. At Super Bowl I, the Los Angeles Coliseum was half-empty, tickets cost as little as $6, and the game opened like a yawn to national TV audiences.

But the nation wasn't tuned out for long.

More people watched the Super Bowl in 1970 than Neil Armstrong's first steps on the moon a few months before.

Super Bowl V became the first to set a TV ratings record for sports. Miami's 24-7 win over Minnesota in XIII was taped and saved for the four astronauts aboard Skylab 3. Pittsburgh's 21-17 win over Dallas in Super Bowl X drew the highest Nielsen share of all time, with 78 percent of all US television sets that were in use.

Super bowl XX was the first to be taped and sent to China, drawing 127 million in the U.S. and 750 million worldwide.

In 1990 the Big One knocked the "Roots" finale off the all-time list of most-viewed TV shows, leaving the third-ranked final "MASH" episode as the only non-Super Bowl program on the list.

At one point, Norman Vincent Peale said, "If Jesus were alive, he'd be here."

By the time Elway made his Super debut, he was insightful enough to realize he was a sidelight.

"It's the media. It's the attention. Look at the stories. Most are about the media. It's the spectacle."

Actually, it's more.

According to Hallmark Cards, Super Sunday generates more social gatherings than any other occasion, including Christmas, Thanksgiving and New Year's Eve, making it America's No. 1 communal rite. It's also white-hot TV, at least to advertisers. The Academy Awards lure older women, the World Series older men, golf the rich. But the Super Bowl drags every sect in the cathode-ray universe — men, women, old, young, rich, poor.

When the 49ers played in Palo Alto in XIX, San Francisco's crime rate dropped nearly 75 percent. Fifteen years before, when the Chiefs played in Super Bowl IV, there was reportedly one burglary in Kansas City, and police waited until halftime to grill the suspect.

By Elway's first Super Bowl, corporations ran commercials to promote their commercials on Super Sunday. The morning after, millions analyze the video ads as passionately as the game itself.

Americans feel they're entitled to good TV. They invented it (virtually). They made it famous. Yet they haven't gotten their due from the Super Bowl. The game itself is "America's Great Script Tease," due in some part to Elway, who was on the wrong end of two of the worst defeats in sports history.

The image of Elway running for his life is a permanent part of Super Bowl lore, along with The Fridge, Roger the Dodger, Mean Joe Green, The Hogs, The Killer B's, The Steel Curtain, The Purple People Eaters, The Doomsday Defense, The No-Name Defense, The Chicago Bears' rapping, Deion Sanders' gemmed fingers, Jim McMahon's headband, Jim Turner's high-tops, Joe Namath's poolside cool, Vince Lombardi's halo, Max McGee's hangover, Scott Haywood's haywire pulse, Doug Williams' pulsating second quarter, John Madden's slovenliness, Al Davis' subversiveness, Johnny Unitas' last hurrah, Bart Starr's first hurrah, Whitney Houston's voice, Duane Thomas' silence, Jim Kelly's endless futility, Jackie Smith's end-zone futility ....

It didn't appear Elway was bound for catastrophe on the eve of Super Bowl XXI.

Before the Broncos departed for Pasadena, more than 63,000 true believers gathered at Mile High Stadium for a send-off rally.

"If you thought last week was good, wait until next week," Elway boomed over the PA system, referring to The Drive. "We've achieved two of our goals; we've got one more to go."

The state was electrified. And goofy.

Copper Mountain ski resort diluted several gallons of industrial-strength food dye and put a huge orange stripe down one of its main ski trails. A local deputy district attorney general wrote an "epic poem" celebrating The Drive. Members of a Boulder church ended Sunday morning service by drinking 2-ounce cups of Orange Crush while praying for a Broncos win.

When he arrived in L.A., Elway was in title overdrive. Less than a decade before, he'd lived down the road from the Rose Bowl, a fact that he and his parents mulled from their Super Bowl suites.

"This is our dream," Jack Elway said.

While Elway was appearing on tape on NBC's "Today Show" early Thursday, his mother was appearing live from San Francisco on ABC's "Good Morning America."

Jack had been on the recruiting trail for Stanford in Portland, Seattle, Boise, San Francisco, Dallas, Houston and then back to San Francisco. He made sure he was available for his son's once-in-a-lifetime Super Bowl, though he believed it would happen more than once.

"I think this is just the first time," Jack told the *Denver Post*. "You talk about Denver and the whole thing, the intensity and everything — it's pretty tough to be lousy. They won't put up with it. Those are damn educated fans; and when you get something like that going, it really plays a role."

John, meanwhile, was on the run.

He limousined to Hollywood to see Eddie Murphy on the set of "Beverly Hills Cop II." He streaked past marquees: "John Elway vs. The Giants." He was surrounded by the newshounds on media day. He out-glittered Giants quarterback Phil Simms.

"I'm not a flash like John Elway; just a lunch bucket kind of guy," Simms said.

As the countdown to game time commenced, Elway finally slowed down, and huddled with his parents and family, the final pause before the game of his life.

"I just enjoy having them around. My father is kind of like my security blanket. I just feel better when both he and my mom are around," John said.

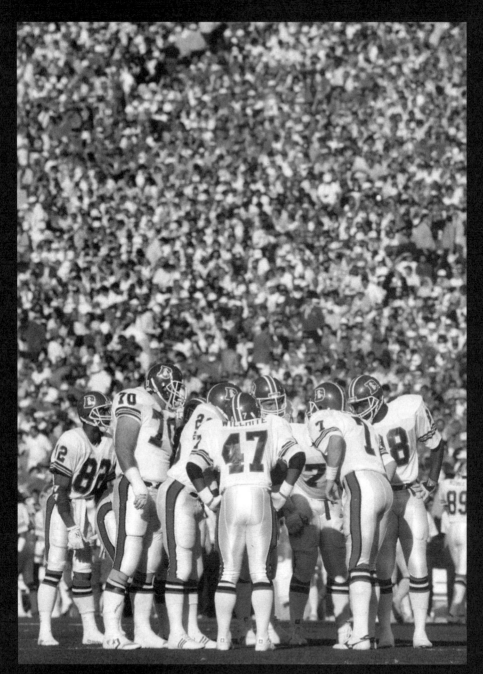

Many insiders say that the Broncos were the closest thing to a one man team in Super Bowl history. Although Keith Bishop, Vance Johnson, Steve Watson and others were more than capable players, the Broncos Super Bowl hopes began and ended with Elway.

"He'll get quiet before a football game, and there isn't anything that needs to be said," the elder Elway said. "I know what it is and I know what I'm like before games. You get quiet and you get reflective. And then all of a sudden there's a period of relief and relaxation before a game. You've done all you can do to prepare, and now it's time for the damn game to start. That can be almost a relief to get on with it.

"This is the ultimate. It's almost too good to be true. It's something you work for. I know this has been John's dream. This is what he's worked for. This is what he wanted to happen."

The game started like a dream for Elway. He drove his team into Giants territory on his first possession, setting up Rich Karlis' 48-yard field goal, which tied a Super Bowl record for distance. The Broncos led 3-0.

Simms came right back, guiding the Giants on a 78-yard scoring drive that ended with his pass to Zeke Mowatt for a 7-3 lead.

Elway countered with a 58-yard scoring drive. He hit Sammy Winder for a 9-yard gain on the six-play drive, and, improvising near the goal line, scored on a 4-yard run. The Broncos led 10-7. In 13 of the previous 20 Super Bowls, there had never even been a lead change. This one had already produced two, and a sense the game might actually live up to its name.

As the second quarter started, the Broncos were on the move again. Relying on his nimble feet once more, Elway left the pocket and then passed deep to Vance Johnson for a 58-yard gain. Within moments, Denver was on the Giants 1, with first down, and a chance to go ahead 17-9.

In all Super Bowls the tension level jumps off the stress charts. Montana has watched the replay of his 92-yard drive to beat Cincinnati in Super Bowl XXIII at least XXIII times. It's the only way he can remember it. "It's a blur," he told *Sports Illustrated*. "I hyperventilated to the point of almost blacking out. You know how a TV screen gets fuzzy. Well, that's what my vision was like. I was yelling so loudly in the huddle that I couldn't breathe. Things got blurrier and blurrier.

"One time I put my hands under center and I felt like it was taking days to call the play. Everything was in slow motion. When I took the first step back, the

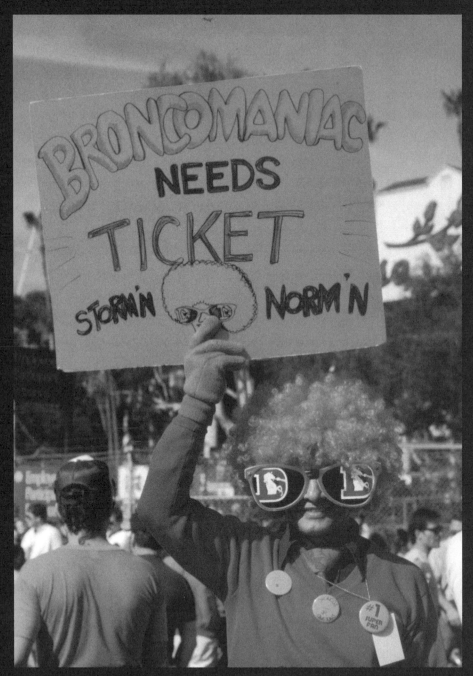

Bronco fans showed up en masse at the Rose Bowl. Before the team headed to L.A., more than 63,000 true believers showed up at Mile High Stadium for a send-off rally, during which Elway proclaimed, "If you thought last week was good, wait until next week."

fuzz appeared again. By the fifth step, things got so fuzzy I had to throw the ball over Jerry Rice, out of bounds, to clear my head."

San Francisco cornerback Eric Wright started crying on the sideline at the Pontiac Silverdome during pre-game introductions at Super Bowl XVI.

"I was so keyed up, so juiced, that I lost it," he said. "My body chemistry totally changed. I had no appetite that day. I was sharp, on edge. Any little thing some-body said, I fired back. 'Leave me alone.' All my emotions were on the surface."

Elway, however, was as cool as a California breeze at the Rose Bowl. He had the ball on the 1, the world in his hand.

On first down, Elway rolled to the right, looking to pass, but Lawrence Taylor grounded him for a 1-yard loss. On the next play, Elway tried a trap with Gerald Willhite. It didn't work. Harry Carson dumped him for no gain. Since the Broncos hadn't been able to produce brute-force running yards all season, Reeves could've sent in wideouts to spread the field. But he chose to leave the big guys on the field against a defense that limited Denver to 14 rushing yards in the first half.

On third and two, Elway pitched to Sammy Winder, who tried to go wide. Carl Banks dumped him on the 6-yard line.

Instead of gaining a 17-7 lead, and ultimate momentum, the Broncos had to set-tle for a Rich Karlis field-goal attempt.

They had to settle for less. Karlis, 11-of-12 from inside the 39 to that point, blew a 23-yard chip shot, which blew away the Broncos. From the moment of that goal-line failure, Denver didn't attempt another run until midway through the final quarter.

As the half ended, Karlis missed a 34-yard kick — to the right again.

At intermission, the Broncos led 10-9, and Elway was 13 of 20 for 187 yards. But only the husks of his dreams remained.

The Giants scored the first three times they had the ball in the third quarter, the Broncos couldn't manage a first down, and the rout was on.

As the Giants increased their lead to 16-10, 19-10, 26-10, 33-10, Elway was

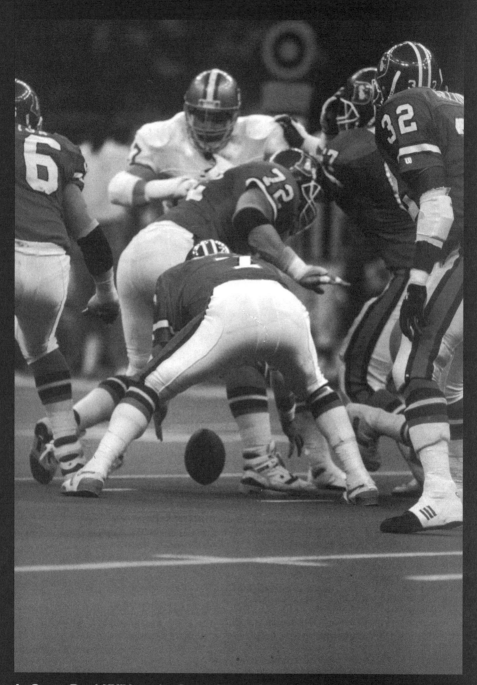

In Super Bowl XXIV at the Superdome, Elway never got untracked. His first pass was wildly underthrown. Near the end, he dropped the ball while being sacked. San Francisco's Daniel Stubbs picked it up and ran to the 1. Roger Craig scored on the next play, giving the 49ers a 55-10 lead.

reeling. In downtown Denver, nearly 1,500 people had gathered to watch on a 28x16-foot television screen. Only a few die-hards remained by the fourth quarter.

At the Rose Bowl, the "Bronco Bunny" — superfan Shirley Gorman — stood alone in an exit tunnel.

"I'm so sad. I'm stunned. I really am. I don't know what happened," she said.

Then she began crying.

Elway felt like doing the same. He was supposed to be the quarterback throwing bombs and perfect darts with graceful gusto.

He was supposed to be the guy being canonized, not diminished in the twilight aftermath.

Instead, Elway headed to the press room with a morose stare, wearing a white terrycloth robe, looking entirely like a defeated heavyweight champion.

"I felt like I did everything I could," he said. "I gave 110 percent. I think I got all out of myself I could.

"It hurts when we didn't get into the end zone on first-and-goal.

"In the second half, they beat us. There's nothing else to it. They played great football."

So did Elway, especially in the first half, when he had been everything the Giants feared. He ran for a touchdown. He passed for a touchdown. He ran left and threw 54 yards down to the right, and almost scored another touchdown.

But Phil Simms, who completed 22-of-25 passes for 268 yards and three touchdowns during the Giants' 39-20 win, was headed to Disneyland. And Elway to Miseryland.

"That might be the best game a quarterback has ever played," Giants coach Bill Parcells said of his man.

The Super Bowl is a place of atonement, as Simms had shown. He'd been booed by New Yorkers when it was announced the Giants had drafted him. Too many times fans had thrown snow balls, decaying fruit and loads of verbal abuse at Simms, who'd been benched, ridiculed, mocked, derided and reviled without mercy, and, at times, reason.

Terry Bradshaw also found atonement on Super Sunday. His name and game spelled disgrace. During a press conference preceding his third victory, a team-mate, lineman Jon Kolb, tried to set the record straight about his buddy. In his colorful book, *Super Bowl Chronicles,* Jerry Green reports that Kolb talked of the night he and Bradshaw had spent at a jamboree in Wheeling, West Virginia. They wanted to drive back to Pittsburgh, but couldn't break free from some lingering fans.

An official led them out a back alley and to an escape route.

"I'm probably doing Terry a disservice by telling this," Kolb said. "My job is to protect him, after all. I don't think he wants it known.

"We came out of the jamboree in Wheeling. We were among all those people, then suddenly we were with nobody. There was this man in the alley. I don't know if he had a weapon and was going to use it on himself. I didn't search him. But he was depressed.

"He told Terry what he was going to do. He said, 'I'm going to kill myself.' Terry talked him out of it. He talked to him for a half-hour, one-on-one. I know that. I don't know what he said. I was so cold I went to the car to wait.

"You know, so many people malign Terry. They don't know him."

After the Steelers' 35-31 win over the Cowboys, Bradshaw said with a wink, "I was nervous as a cat."

Elway sought atonement 12 months after his first Black Sunday. He knew that to be a truly great quarterback, you must win the ultimate game. "That's on my mind. In my career, the ultimate is to win this game"

Reeves had once tried to motivate the Broncos by stacking greenbacks on a table. For this game, he exhibited championship rings.

Elway exhibited cool. During media day, he wore blue-tinted sunglasses, white shoes, with laces untied, and chomped on gum. When the 45-minute session ended, Elway said, "Time flies when you're having fun".

Jerry Green recounted in *Super Bowl Chronicles* that a persistent reporter had asked, "The game's in Jack Murphy Stadium. John, do you know who Jack Murphy was?"

"No," Elway said.

"He was a sportswriter."

"He must never have written a bad thing to have a stadium named after him," Elway said.

Like Simms the year before, Elway's opposite — Washington quarterback Doug Williams — was regarded as the second best quarterback in the Super Bowl. Williams was the first black quarterback to start in the Super Bowl, turning the game into a sociological event, especially when CBS's Jimmy the Greek applied his own historical perspective.

"The black is the better athlete, and he practices to be the better athlete, and he's bred to be the better athlete because all this goes back to the slave period," Jimmy the Greek said. "The slave owner would breed this big black with this big woman so he could have a big black kid. That's where it all started."

Once again, Elway led the Broncos to an early lead. On the first play, he and Ricky Nattiel teamed for a 56-yard touchdown pass. On the second possession he put Karlis in position for a 24-yard field goal on the next series. The Broncos led 10-0.

"We're up 10-0. We really had momentum," Elway said. "Then it caved in. It was my (No. 1) disappointment."

On the third possession, Elway drove the team into Redskins territory once more, moving to the 30 where they faced third and 10. Redskins safety Alvin Walton raced through the line and sacked Elway for an 18-yard loss.

"The momentum really seemed to shift there," Reeves said.

Talk about an understatement.

Although he had been sidelined in the first quarter, Williams returned for anoth-

The 49ers repeatedly brought Elway to his knees which helps explain why
he completed only 10-of-26 passes for 108 yards. None went for a TD.
On the first pass of the second half, he was picked off by Michael Walter.
On the next play, Joe Montana threw a 28-yard scoring pass.

er shot — actually five of 'em. In the greatest single-quarter production in football history, Williams burned the Broncos for five touchdowns.

In a span of 13:03 and 18 plays, using only 5:47 of the clock, Williams completed 11 passes in the quarter for 228 yards and touchdowns of 80, 27, 50 and eight yards. Before the half was over, the Redskins had piled up 419 yards, 356 in the second quarter alone.

"It was like dreamland," Washington offensive tackle R.C. Thielemann said.

Williams knelt down on a knee to run the clock out. As Michael Jackson's "Bad" poured out of the loud-speakers, the Broncos stumbled into their locker room for intermission.

The second half allowed Americans a chance to catch up with their sleep. Elway rifled through his file cards on comebacks, then gave in to reality.

Williams finished the day with a Super-Bowl record 340 yards passing and was named the game's Most Valuable Player.

Elway?

He wasn't a one-man team this time. He was just as bad as his teammates: 38 passes, 14 completions, three interceptions, five sacks. And too cool, some teammates said.

"John didn't scream at anybody," wide receiver Mark Jackson said. "He plays better when he's screaming at people. Usually, if you screw up, he'll tell you. And we were really screwing up. For some reason, he didn't go crazy. John was too controlled today."

Added guard Keith Bishop: "John didn't say anything when the game was slipping away. And he didn't say anything at halftime. I just figured there were some things he couldn't control, and John knew it."

Elway controlled his emotions in the press conference afterward.

Asked if he's ever suffered a worse defeat, he said, "Uh-huh, last year."

On what play did the momentum shift?

"Second quarter," he said.

What play helped the Redskins?

"Second quarter," he said.

When did you realize ...

"Second quarter."

What phase of the game did they take away from you?

"Our passing game."

Not too far away, Bronco's owner Pat Bowlen expressed the sentiments of many in the organization.

"Having your butts kicked and being embarrassed in the Super Bowl is a major, major disappointment," he said in the depths of Jack Murphy Stadium. "You look down there, see the other team score 35 unanswered points, and you've got to look at the different schemes and say, 'What the hell is going on out there?'"

When Elway bitterly complained about media suffocation the following season, Bowlen said another factor induced Elway's malaise.

"When you go to the Super Bowl twice and you lose it, psychologically you feel you've lost two opportunities to achieve that crown jewel in your career, ... I think that, more than anything, is going through John's mind. Losing two Super Bowls, feeling there's a void in his career ... I think he's being hard on himself."

Before the start of the 1989 season, Elway increased his running and weight-lifting regimens. Some said he had a zealous look as he prepared for Season No. 7.

"To see him come in five times a week in the off-season, two or three hours a day, to me the driving force is we've gotten beat in two Super Bowls," Reeves said. "When you get beat in two championship games like that, it hurts, and if you're a competitor, it really hurts."

"I don't know how I'd handle it if I didn't win it," Elway said. "I won't feel totally complete when I get out of it. You don't feel totally satisfied if you don't have one. But I'm still going to walk away from the game feeling like I did have success. Hell, I feel lucky I've been there."

But during an interview with *Rocky Mountain News* beat writer Rick Morrissey, Fran Tarkenton said that he'd never been able to shake the effects of three Super Bowl defeats.

"The failure of those three days, that I had a chance to play in that game, the ultimate game in pro football, and not winning. I haven't learned to deal with it, quite frankly," he said.

"... I've heard other people say they accept it as life, but I can't. I wish I could. It absolutely bothers me that I've never been able to live it down. And the sad part is that I don't have a tomorrow. I can't go back out there (now). But I've had dreams of going back and playing at 46 and age 43 and 42, and in the back of my mind I still think I could if someone would give me the chance. And that's sick, but that's how much it bothers me. I wish I could cope with it and deal with it. But I really haven't been able to do it."

Earl Morrall was the losing quarterback to Joe Namath in Super Bowl III, which overnight made the American Football League and NFL equal partners. By not guiding the Baltimore Colts to victory, Morrall felt he'd let more than himself and his team down.

"I still get flashbacks about what happened ... I've played the whole game over in my mind. I've wished thousands of times to do that game over again, because what went wrong was my fault," he said.

Entering the AFC Championship game against Cleveland, Elway was riding high. Bobby Humphrey was a first-rate runner, and the defense, though new and relatively untested at the start of the season, was the best in several years.

"I think in '86 and '87, it was to some extent John Elway and 10 other guys," Bowlen said. "I mean, he's still a very, very big part of this football team, but I think he has a much bigger supporting staff. I can't think back to a quarterback who's won a Super Bowl without a pretty good supporting cast."

But Elway said his role was basically the same as it'd always been.

"When it's third and six, they're not looking to Bobby Humphrey. They're still looking at me."

The Browns were obsessed with Elway. Tension had been building for a week in the owners' suites. Browns owner Art Modell had refused to sit in Denver's visiting owner's box in the AFC Championship game two years before, calling it a "disgrace." He rented another luxury box for $5,000. At that same title game, Modell had complained when Reeves appeared alone on the cover of what was supposed to be an unbiased game-day program. For the 1990 game, the Broncos put out an unbiased cover — with a picture of Reeves holding the disputed cover from two years before.

After Elway had guided the Broncos to a 37-21 win, Modell was the picture of deportment. "What a magnificent performance," he said of Elway. "It's equal to Unitas, Namath, Graham — anyone over the years."

Elway completed 20 of 36 passes for 385 yards and three touchdowns. In the first half, he rolled right, and then, as Cleveland's Clay Matthews closed in on him, threw the ball off the wrong foot, side-armed, for a 70-yard TD.

In the second half, after the Browns had cut the deficit to 24-21, Elway threw a perfect strike on the run, both across and down field, for a 39-yard touchdown to Sammy Winder.

"I was all over him," said Cleveland defensive end Al Baker. "And then he throws an out-of-the-shoulder-socket pass all the way across the field. All day he was outrunning guys with 4.4 and 4.5 speed. If he keeps this up, I'm going to have to be a John Elway fan."

Following the win, the Broncos took a victory lap.

It turned out to be Denver's last hurrah, as fans feared. Before the AFC title game, a TV station asked viewers: Do you want the Broncos to go to Super Bowl XXIV?

They voted 1500 to 1300 to stay home.

A few days before the game, a headline in the *Rocky Mountain News* read: "Denverites fear shame — again; Dread of loss dilutes hopes of fame, glory."

By then, psychologists were busy preparing fans for Public Issue 1A: How to deal with another "Blue Monday."

Elway was infuriated.

"For me to be the quarterback I want to be, we've got to win this game," Elway said before Super Bowl XXIV. But it wasn't to be. By halftime, he was just six-for-20. By game's end, he was ashen-faced. "This is going to live with me."

"Why don't those people go hide in their closets. They're taking the easy way out. If we lose, we lose, but I'd hate to be stuck in the closet," he said.

He might have had second thoughts a few days later.

During a routine press conference in New Orleans, Terry Bradshaw carved up Elway.

"I think John's problem is he's been babied by the fans, the media, and, to an extent, by the coaches. It's really too easy for him," Bradshaw said.

"Is he a great quarterback? Nope. A good one. When you choose a profession, and if you don't reach the pinnacle, you can't consider yourself a success ... He's too inconsistent. He lets too many things bother him. He's got to get a little tougher emotionally."

Elway fired back: "Terry Bradshaw has been bashing me since I got in the league. He didn't like the money I make. He still doesn't. He can stick it in his ear."

But signs of doom lurked at every turn.

During a Thursday practice in the Superdome, Reeves noticed that officials had painted all the previous Super Bowl competitors on the rim of the mezzanine, with the winning team's helmet first, to the left side, and the losers to the right.

"They had Super Bowl XXIV up there with the place for the score blank," Reeves said, "and they already had a San Francisco helmet painted on the left and a Denver helmet painted on the right. They expect us to lose."

That was a crushing thought to Elway.

"For me to be the quarterback I want to be, we've got to win this game," he said.

This time, Elway didn't get off to a fast start; he never got started at all. On the first possession, he fired two passes wildly into the ground, and the Broncos punted. On the second possession, he moved them to the 25, and misfired three more times. The Broncos swapped nervous glances.

In the second quarter, Elway continued to struggle. By halftime, he was six-for-

20 and the 49ers led 27-3.

On his first pass of the second half, Elway was intercepted by the 49ers' Michael Walter. On the play after that, Joe Montana hit Jerry Rice on a 28-yard scoring pass. San Francisco led 34-3. On the Broncos' next possession, Chet Brooks picked off an Elway pass and returned it 38 yards. Montana and John Taylor connected on a 35-yard scoring toss to increase the 49ers' lead to 41-3.

Later, Elway was sacked, dropped the ball, San Francisco's Daniel Stubbs picked it up and ran to the Broncos' 1-yard line. Roger Craig scored on the next play, increasing the Niners' lead to 55-10.

In a game played on a world stage, Elway's numbers were humiliating: 26 passes, 10 completions, 108 yards, no touchdowns, one interception.

The Broncos were accustomed to humiliating Super Bowl denouements. At the end of Super Bowl XII, when Denver's fabled defense was beaten 27-10 by Dallas, Cowboys linebacker Hollywood Henderson crumpled an orange cup in his fist, threw it at the crowd, and yelled: "That's your Orange Crush."

But this was past belief.

"If I didn't get so tired, I could have played three games. I only got touched twice — once when I scrambled out of bounds — and I didn't get sacked at all," Montana said.

The next day, Elway read his notices.

Both Bradshaw and 49ers defensive back Tim McKyer said Elway couldn't read defenses. Johnny Unitas, the Holy Father of quarterbacks, was just as critical.

"My feeling about John Elway is that he has been, throughout his career, inconsistent," he said. "The reason he throws the ball so hard at times is because he doesn't anticipate the break of his receiver. You read the coverages and anticipate the breaks, then you don't have to beat the defenders because you've already got them there. I don't know that John has improved as much as you would expect. He's an extremely talented athlete, but I think that's the thing that bothers people. I thought his Super Bowl performance was very poor."

Reeves quickly defended his embattled quarterback.

Elway was often on his back in the Superdome. Meanwhile, 49ers quarterback Joe Montana was not sacked once. "I only got touched twice," said Montana who cemented his reputation as one of the greatest quarterbacks in NFL history with his Super Bowl appearances.

"Anybody who would say John can't read defenses can't possibly know what they're talking about," he said. "That's my job. Unless they're coaching him, how the hell are they going to know whether he can read defenses or not? A guy like McKyer just better be glad he's got guys up front rushing the quarterback, or we'd be seeing how well he reads pass routes. Of course, it's hard to beat a guy who's always on the bench.

"I mean, this is so stupid. I don't even want to talk about it. I mean, if he couldn't read defenses, I guarantee you he wouldn't be playing.

"If he reads and wants to believe what people are writing about him or what's being said about him, then you've got to worry about (Elway's confidence). But John is tough enough and he's been around the sport long enough to know that it comes with the territory.

"One of these days the weight that's on his shoulders will be lifted off him."

Fran Tarkenton also came to Elway's defense.

"Do you think that Elway's team has to win a Super Bowl to validate his career? I don't," Tarkenton said. " I think that's the most ridiculous thing."

But Elway was beyond consolation.

"This is going to live with me," he said as he stepped onto the team bus. "I know that."

1989 was the Year of Living Miserably for Elway. He felt increasingly isolated, in part because he couldn't venture out in public without being recognized or talked about. "I can't get it into my mind I'm someone special," he said.

Chapter 6 — "I'm Suffocating"

AS HE TURNED 30, JOHN ELWAY INVENTORIED HIS LIFE.

On the asset side, he had a model wife, healthy kids, a magical name, sterling Q ratings, an MVP trophy, an incipient auto empire, a mountain view, a dog or two, some sports cars, a power golf swing, The Arm, a Rolodex to the stars, an international itinerary, a place in football history and enough time yet to win a Super Bowl ring.

The debit side?

No place to hide.

Elway was living his life in the headlines, which was nothing new. But the cumulative effect of the saturation coverage had increasingly enraged and estranged him from ordinary life. Every time he looked, Elway was being watched and chronicled.

His breath-taking life had become just that.

"I'm about to suffocate," he said.

The detonating event came in 1989. Elway continued to be frustrated by coach Dan Reeve's conservative offense, which sheathed rather than showcased his assets. He anguished over his place in football history, as well as Super Bowl fiascoes.

But Elway reserved his real wrath for the newspapers, talk shows and TV stations that made his life a mile-high inferno.

"You guys are like Attila the Hun of the media," Raiders defensive lineman Howie Long told Denver reporters.

Elway began to avoid his inquisitors entirely. For example, when they sought to question him after Mike Shanahan was re-hired as a Broncos' assistant, Elway hid in the training room, then slipped out a back door and into a get-away car.

"I wanted to be a quarterback here, but it came down to if they painted the building, the media wanted to know what I thought about it," he said. "I was avoiding questions instead of saying 'No.' I just didn't want to answer them. I held a lot of animosity toward (the media) and I didn't want to give them any time. I had been very open with them.

"Somebody gave me a statistic that, out of 365 days in 1988, the Broncos were mentioned in the paper all but three days. That tells you a little about it."

What angered Elway most were unsubstantiated reports that he had a drinking problem — and that the problem was affecting his play. An ESPN reporter confronted him directly about the allegations. Elway, who has never been arrested for public intoxication or driving under the influence, denied he had a problem, and moved on.

But Denver's reluctant star burst a couple weeks later.

"They talk about my hair, they talk about my teeth, they talk about how much I tip, how much I drink, how I'm playing, when I'll talk to the media. I'm sick of it," he told a *Sports Illustrated* reporter following an October loss to the Philadelphia Eagles. "I'm about to suffocate.

"I don't want to sound like a crybaby, so I don't talk about it. But it's just gotten to be too much lately. I'm just torn up inside right now."

Would he like to be traded?

"I don't know."

Would he like to quit?

"I don't know."

How much more is he willing to take?

"Not much."

Would he like to not talk to the media?

"Yeah, but nobody in this organization would let me do it."

Would he like to leave town?

"We bought a place in Palm Springs and we're going to get away more often now."

That same weekend, Eagles coach Buddy Ryan took a shot. "People used to compare Randall Cunningham to John Elway, now they compare Elway to Randall," Ryan said.

Said Elway: "Just another day in Beat Up John Elway Week."

Elway didn't go his own unsweet way. *Rocky Mountain News* columnist Jay Mariotti shot back, calling him "a greedy and scared punk ... Go ahead John, leave. Get out of Denver, baby. Go. You'll be crawling back here after a week."

The *Rocky Mountain News'* switchboard nearly caught fire because of infuriated callers, as did the Broncos', which received 350 calls in support of Elway, including one from Denver's mayor.

Mariotti was doing his radio show at a local restaurant when he noticed four policemen approaching. As they surrounded him, Mariotti was told two death threats had been phoned in. In a city where a prominent radio talk-show host had been gunned down, these calls aren't easily dismissed.

"My contention in my column was that he's smothering himself," Mariotti explained. "He does so much on the side that the media isn't smothering him. He's smothering himself with his profit-making ventures. I became infuriated with a smear job on the media because all in all, if you compare it to Philadelphia and New York, we've pretty much laid off him. We don't smother him."

Broncos owner Pat Bowlen waded into the angry stew, focusing on *Sports Illustrated* writer Rick Reilly, a Denver resident and multi-winner of the national sportswriter of the year award.

"I think we all know what kind of articles Rick Reilly writes," Bowlen said. "He wrote the article regarding (the University of Colorado) and the problem with the players up there. He wrote Brian Bosworth's book, so he's kind of the resident director of smut for Sports Inquirer. That's the way I look at it."

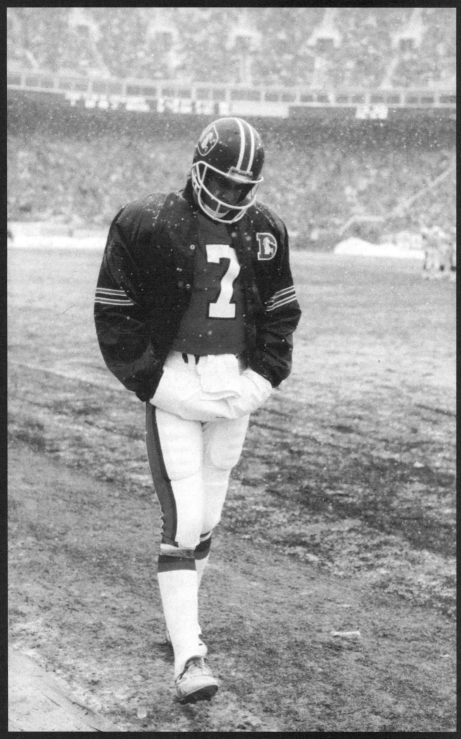

During much of the 1989 season, Elway found himself under siege on and off the field. Philadelphia coach Buddy Ryan said Randall Cunningham, his quarterback, had surpassed Elway, who fumed in silence until he could hold back no more.

Referring to a bicycle accident Bowlen had been involved in, Reilly said, "The only thing I can figure is that Pat must have suffered more brain damage in the bicycle accident than we figured.

"I really don't understand where Pat's coming from, because I never heard anything from Elway or Reeves to indicate they had a problem with the story. If anything, I got the impression that it was something that needs to be said."

The Elway media wars were benign, at least by some standards. Pittsburgh Steelers defensive tackle Mean Joe Green spit in a reporter's face in 1970. In 1989, Jim McMahon, then playing for San Diego, blew his nose on a beat writer. Dale Robertson of the *Houston Post* got in an acerbic exchange with Oilers quarterback Dan Pastorini a couple days before the 1980 AFC Championship game. Pastorini pushed him through a half-open door leading to a practice field. They landed at the feet of Oilers coach Bum Phillips, who had been elaborating in an interview how well his team got along with the local media. New York Jets quarterback Richard Todd pushed *New York Post* reporter Steve Serby into a wall, cutting Serby's nose. The *Post* headline ran: "Todd Assaults our Man," with an adjoining picture of Serby, a bandage on his nose.

Elway has managed to avoid embarrassment. He was insightful enough to foresee the consequences of a public misdeed, and how it might appear on Eyewitness News.

"I've thought about those things," he said. "That's why I'm so careful of it. It doesn't matter. If you're in the headlines, you're wrong. Unless somebody is assaulting my wife or my family, I'm never going to get involved in a situation like that.

"People are always going to have something to say, but I'm able to walk away from those things. I have to."

After Elway's big blowup, he met with an NFL security representative.

"I just wanted to ask him what we can do to hopefully cut everything down to where we can all be on the same page. The bottom line is, I want to be able to go and have a drink somewhere, whether it's a Coca-Cola or a Coors light. I'd like ...

to be able to give out candy without Denver knowing what we're giving out. That's something I'm getting fed up with."

Bill Malone, the NFL rep, said, "As far as I'm concerned, John's a class guy. The allegations are tied into whether the Broncos win or lose. If they lose, there are a lot more. We get these allegations with a lot of players, not just John."

As it turned out, the controversy served as a catalyst for a successful season that culminated with another Super Bowl appearance. And more stories about Elway, Colorado's leading man.

"I can't get it in my mind that I'm someone special," he said. "In my mind I'm still the same old John Elway."

But he wasn't the same old John — anywhere.

In the mid-80s, Elway was on the back streets of Mazatlan, Mexico, soaking in the soothing oblivion of ordinary life — like any other leisurely American in search of some passing fun. For a few minutes, at least.

"We're in a ghetto, nobody speaks English, and all of a sudden a little Mexican boy yells, 'John Elway, John Elway, John Elway!,'" recalled Steve Watson.

In the wide, wide, world of sports, Elway had gone global. Over the years, the Broncos have played in international pre-season games six times, tying them with the San Francisco 49ers for most mileage-plus points. Elway was hot copy in Barcelona, Berlin, Tokyo (twice) and London, where he outdrew soccer super-star Diego Maradona, in a country where football will always mean soccer. "I believe John Elway is the greatest attraction in sports today," said a London cab driver, who'd taken his son to see Elway play in the quarterback's Super Bowl debut.

"My son thinks Elway is the greatest quarterback ever. It was amazing to see my boy sit there for three hours, totally absorbed. He never got up to use the bathroom. I was bringing him Cokes and popcorn, and he never got up. He was fascinated. American football has more excitement, more passion than any of our sports."

Added another Londoner: "Elway's a giant. What is he, 6-6? I've heard he can throw the ball from the back of one end zone to the back of the other."

Elway was a media darling for Fleet Street's most inquiring scribes.

Q — "Are you always being recognized?"

A — "Yeah, especially in Denver."

Q — "How do you cope with that?"

A — "It's tough, your private life deteriorates because your face is in the paper quite a bit, so we're easily recognizable"

Q — "Do you have this sort of thing where other guys try to take you on?"

A — "No, they just want an autograph or want to say 'Hi.'"

Q — "So you don't go out very much?"

A — "Every once in a while."

Q — "And watch television?"

A — "You bet — the telly."

Q — "How many set plays are there that you have to remember?"

A — "We'll probably go into a game with between 60 and 80 set plays."

Q — "How on Earth do you remember them all? Do you write them all down in a book, or what?"

A — "It's just like history in school. Once you learn it, it's hard to forget. That's why it gets easier every year I'm in the league"

Q — "And what about signals? Do you change signals every week?"

A — "No, we haven't had anybody who picks up our signals yet, so we haven't had to change them."

Q — "What are they?"

A — "If I told you, we'd have to change them."

Q — "Can you imagine the Super Bowl ever being played here?"

A — "I think you'd have an awful lot of people in the U.S. mad about it."

Q — "But it's an international venue. You wouldn't have any sectionalism."

A — "Yeah, but it's an American game."

Elway had his share of fun in London, whooping it up on a pub crawl through London, including a punk-rock club in Coventry Gardens, where he and his linemen partied hardy.

"One guy had a hat on his head shaped like a vacuum cleaner," guard Keith Bishop said. "Elway tried to buy it from the guy for 100 pounds. But the guy wouldn't sell it. He told John, 'I'm making a statement with this.'"

Londoners were beguiled by Elway; Japanese obsessed.

In the main shopping district in 1990, at the NFL's newest retail outlet, Elway was engulfed by pressing fans.

"It was alarming, it was claustrophobic," Jim Saccomano, director of media relations, said.

It also was another indication of Elway's tremendous drawing power.

"Just the volume of mail he receives is staggering," Saccomano said. "I remember one day walking through the locker room and there were orange crates sitting next to his locker. I said, 'Whoa, what the heck is this?' Then I looked through 'em and they were filled with mail.

"John is the classic superstar. He's changed the Denver Broncos into an international club."

These days, Elway receives about 40,000 autograph requests a year, as well as desperate pleas for cash, cars and heroic deeds. He must change his phone number every couple months. And in public, he keeps his head down and eyes enwrapped in sunglasses.

Saccomano said, "I could call Jay Leno right now and say, 'Jay, Elway's going to be in L.A. tomorrow, and he wants to be on the show.' Trust me, he'd find the room. He has standing invitations from Letterman, 'The Today Show'. 'Good Morning America'."

In 1993, Elway checked into the team hotel in Appleton, Wisconsin, then hurried to a meeting.

Upon leaving, Elway walked into a spontaneous convention of autograph-seekers. After scribbling his name on a few notebooks, Elway escaped into an elevator. As the door closed, a bridesmaid from an adjacent wedding party pleaded for him to salute the bride and groom.

Elway shook his head, the door closed, and that was that. Except Elway was seized by a wave of guilt. Within minutes, he was at the center of the bridal party, posed for cameras.

"For most people, Elway is the way we'd like to see all our stars," said Alan Friedman, a spokesman for Team Marketing, a Chicago company that analyzes marketing trends.

"No one has ever accused him of being a prima donna. He's a strong family man who has played hard and worked hard, and in one city. It's how people want stars to be."

Added Colin Hagen, a senior licensing manager for NFL properties: "He's the antithesis of the aloof, arrogant superstar."

In every poll of America's best-known jocks, Elway ranks among the leaders, along with Troy Aikman, Jerry Rice, Dan Marino, Michael Jordan and Wayne Gretsky. To marketing people, however, Elway transcends the NFL. Seventy percent of the American public knows of Elway, who is a seven-time *Sports Illustrated* cover boy. And since 1986, the Broncos have appeared on more nationally televised games than any club except the 49ers, who happened to win three Super Bowls during that span.

But not all fans are Elway-friendly.

"You wouldn't believe how many people come up and tell me they lost money on us in the Super Bowl," he said. "I say, 'Well, first of all, you shouldn't have bet on it. And second of all, you didn't lose nearly as much as I lost.'"

On the road, Elway is often booed by fans who still regard him as "The Rich Brat who ate Baltimore and then spit it out for something better."

"People still remember that," he said. "With all that hullabaloo that I came out with, that's one of the reasons I'm still getting booed on the road. I bucked the system ... It's like I'm a spoiled brat, that kind of thing.

"Plus, I think booing is the in thing to do these days. Look at baseball and all the run-ins players are having with fans. Fans yelling at players seem to be escalating."

In Denver, however, Elway remains the Main Man. In 1991, after scoring a touchdown, he ran over and gave the ball to a fan in a wheelchair. The Broncos were penalized for Elway's act, which, according to NFL rules, qualified as "excessive celebration."

But the fan beamed.

"I kind of felt like I was The Man," he said.

One of Elway's biggest fans, a resident of Kansas, "wrote a million times trying to meet Elway" after a game against the Kansas City Chiefs. He finally did. That wasn't enough. He and his mother drove more than 700 miles in their Honda Accord with 2MileHI personalized Kansas license plates.

"I'm not an autograph-seeker who goes out and sells the stuff. I live to see the Denver Broncos and be in their footsteps. I live and breathe 'em," the fan said.

The fan's girlfriend dumped him when "I bought my mom a satellite dish so she can watch the Broncos games every Sunday. She (the girlfriend) didn't like to watch football."

"That was devastating," his mother said. "But you have to choose your priorities. His was the Broncos, and her's wasn't."

The attention can get a little much.

When Elway forgets where he has his dinner, he can consult the papers. "John Elway ... and a party of 15 ate at The Palm ... John knocked down a 3-pound lobster and a Porterhouse Steak."

When Janet wants to recount her week, she can look at the Sunday papers. "Janet Elway drove up to the Park Meadows valet stand in John's red Viper convertible for five hours of shopping."

To avoid the autograph-seeking masses, Elway usually eats at places where he knows the owner, so he can slip in and out a side door. When he goes to a movie, Janet buys the tickets while he waits in the car, then John hurries in at the last moment. When he makes a quick stop at a convenience store, it becomes a long inconveniencing one because of the swarming faithful. When Elway's son was born, a newsman asked Saccomano when the birth occurred. "Oh, 2 or 3 in the morning," was the answer. "Gee," the newsman said. "I wish we'd known. We would've sent someone there for pictures."

Sometimes it gets semi-real. In 1987, following threats to Elway's life, 12 officers were stationed behind the Denver bench. Seven accompanied him off the field.

"He fights to have a normal life," Saccomano said. "He wants to be a regular guy. But what can he do?"

Elway can escape in movies (anything involving Glenn Close, John Wayne, Jean Claude Van Damme), books (Tom Clancy), watching sports (baseball, hockey, golf) and following his favorite athlete (Greg Norman).

Sometimes he heads to his log cabin in the Colorado mountains, and wild rides on his snowmobile, or goes camping at a southern Colorado reservoir, or soaks in the sun from his Palm Springs home.

One time he escaped to Germany where he escaped notice.

"Nobody knew me," he said. "It was the first time in a long, long time that I was in a situation where people would look at me and walk right past me. I could walk down a crowded street and have some ales and some bratwurst, and nobody noticed."

"If there's one thing I'd change, it's having people stare at you. I'd like to be able to turn the switch off when I go into public and just be one of the normal people."

No way, Elway. When he attends his daughter's softball games or son's little league game, autograph-seekers run to him.

Jessica, his eldest daughter, turned to her mother once and said: "Mom, who do you think has a harder time with Dad being famous. Him or us?"

After an AFC West road game, Elway was standing in front of his locker, engulfed by layers of reporters and TV cameramen jostling for position, much like NBA power forwards in search of rebounds. Only less athletically.

Behind him, his son watched the pressing mob in stunned silence.

But Elway has it easy compared to Troy Aikman. At the start of his NFL career, Aikman's life seemed as normal as Main Street. He was a celebrated figure in Dallas, but no more than the average Cowboys' star.

Now, following Super Bowl titles, Aikman buys groceries by E-mail, shops at department stores after hours, and for casual conversation checks into computer chat rooms — under a fake name.

He's been stalked by several women, one of whom accused him of turning her into a prostitute, another who ended up in jail, and two who swam in his pool late at night after sneaking onto his property.

Elway never became a total recluse. From his second year in Denver, his wife Janet helped him bear the more unbearable moments. Janet, a world-class swimmer during her Stanford days, understands the wear and tear of athletic ambition.

In fact, in the Elway home, part of the trophy case is reserved for the woman of the house. In 1978, when she was still a high school junior in Tacoma, Washington, she set an American record of 4:52.95 for the 400-meter individual medley in a 25-meter pool. The next year, just as she was about to enter Stanford, she set a World University Games record in the 400 individual medley,

Elway's physical feats are regarded with reverence in countries where football barely has a foothold. Here he talks to a Tokyo broadcaster.

this time in a 50-meter pool, of 5:06.65. In her freshman year, she was a high-point scorer for first-place Stanford in the 1980 National Championships.

John and Janet met at Stanford because a teammate on her swimming team had a crush on John. "I remember saying, 'He's not that cute.' Janet said. "John was well-known at Stanford, but it wasn't a big deal, probably because it seems like everyone at Stanford is a star. My roommate's father was an astronaut — you know, things like that. So being the star of the football team doesn't really set you apart."

During the early years in Denver, Janet was stunned by the hostility level of her husband's critics, who numbered in the tens of thousands.

"When we got married I knew he'd be a public figure, but I had no idea. When I would go into a department store or grocery store and sign a check, they would say, well, not good things about John."

When John threw five interceptions against Kansas City, the crowd threw a fit. "There was this guy sitting right behind me who just wouldn't let up," she recalled for the book *The Color Orange* by Russell Martin. "Finally, he yelled, 'Hey Elway, you can get your g.d. wife pregnant but you can't complete a so-and-so pass.' I turned around and slapped him across the face. He was pretty shocked and I wasn't very proud of myself for doing it, but ... They forget the players and their families are real people, too.

"What he went through that first year was incredible. He would call and tell me things that amazed me. They wanted to know every little thing about him. I'm sure one of the reasons we decided to get married when both of us were still so young was because of what his life was like."

Janet proved to be a stabilizing force for John both on and off the field.

"I can read John's moods and aggressions. I know when he gets home and when he doesn't want to talk," she said.

Because of their parents' athletic backgrounds, it seemed inevitable that the Elway children would be athletically gifted, although Janet was concerned about the pressure the Elway name might impose long before it became a real concern.

"There's always the possibility that we might have one who wants to be an oboe player or something like that," she told the *Denver Post* in 1984. "As long as they can find something they want to devote themselves to, we both would be inclined to help keep them in that direction.

"John and I both have fond memories of our sports activities ... but we both remember friends who were pushed and prodded and began to dislike their sport and started planning ways to evade practice, and eventually began to resent their parents."

When Janet was in junior high, and her progress in swimming sluggish, she wanted to quit to become a cheerleader. But her mother persuaded her to pursue her original dream.

"When I did, and all the dreams began coming true, and I got to travel abroad and try out for the Olympics, I was so thankful that my mom could see farther down the road than I and kept me from quitting," Janet said.

Together, the Elways made a wary peace with the media. In fact, after the third Super Bowl defeat, Elway returned to training camp with a new and liberated view of the fourth estate and the fans who made up his empire.

"I used to think, 'Hey I'm a football player, I'm here to win football games and that's it,'" he said. "I've come to grips with it, and learned to enjoy it, and not fight it. Since that game, I've been able to start enjoying things and realizing that everybody I look at doesn't think I'm a loser. Maybe a couple years ago I'm sitting there thinking that I want everyone thinking that I'm a good quarterback. I want to be ranked No. 1 by everybody. But I've grown up now."

Skeptics suggested Elway's transformation had more to do with his growing business interests, especially car sales.

In fact, after breaking into the auto business, he purposely raised his public profile. His mentor was Pat Bowlen, who was part-owner of a dealership. Elway agreed to do promotions in lieu of up-front capital, while receiving partial ownership.

"No risk involved, and I got to know a little bit about the car business," he said.

"When I first got here, once I got settled in town and settled with my football career, I knew there was something I would eventually get into," Elway, an economics major at Stanford, told *Colorado Business Magazine*. "I never knew exactly what it was. I was hoping that someday it would jump up and grab me. I was fortunate. The car business kind of jumped up and grabbed me."

In 1991, Elway bought a Mazda dealership with Bowlen and Rod Buscher, the only car man in the trio.

Four months later, Buscher and Elway made the largest buyout in the state's automobile history when they added three more dealerships. At that point, Bowlen stepped aside because of a potential conflict of interest with his quarterback.

Elway was majority owner and chairman; Buscher president.

"He had the financial ability and the name, and I had the background in the business, so our partnership was a good marriage," Buscher told *Colorado Business*.

Two years later, Elway's five dealerships sold over 7,500 cars, helping his company gross nearly $130 million in car sales for Honda, Toyota, Oldsmobile, Hyundai and Mazda.

The Elway dealership was one of 10 nationwide to receive Honda's "Master of Total Customer Satisfaction Award," and his Toyota dealership was the only one in the western region to receive the company's top award.

"The car business kind of has a bad reputation," Elway said. "With my name on the building, we're going to take care of the customer first. And we're not going to worry about the extra dollar. We're going to worry about taking care of them and having them as a customer for life.

"The car business is a lot like football in that you've got to do it every day. You can go out and play a great football game on Sunday, the next week fall on your face against somebody you should beat, and you're back into the mediocre level. You've got to stay on top of it and work hard, day in and day out.

"Plus it's competitive. You've got other dealers and so you're competing against them, to be the best. I enjoy the competition. Playing quarterback you develop leadership qualities ... because you're kind of the guy in charge out there on the field on offense, the same way in the car business in the position that I have. I've got to be a leader for everyone else and show them how we want to treat people."

During the season, Elway makes an office stop at least once a day. And he inundates Denver air-waves with self-deprecatory commercials which poke fun at his "endearing" foibles.

"It gives the public a better idea of who I am," Elway said. "People often see me as a highly paid athlete and draw conclusions from that. I don't look at myself that way. I look at the world through my eyes. And to my eyes I look like everyone else."

By 1996, Elway also began to eye a political career. In the spring of '97, he met with Colorado's Republican delegation, ostensibly to discuss "the process."

Elway described himself as a free-market capitalist.

But he'd been eliminated from the rolls in 1993 after failing to vote in the two previous elections. When the *Rocky Mountain News* reported that he'd be ineligible to vote for the proposed Broncos stadium tax, Elway quickly registered as a Republican.

"I said he would get the surprise of his life if he ever ran because he'd go from 100 percent positive name identification to 50 percent positive and 50 percent negative, right after he took his first position on anything," Senator Ben Nighthorse Campbell told the *News*.

"That's the way it works. Everything is downhill from the day you announce ... No matter what you say, somebody doesn't like it."

Nonetheless, Colorado is expected to gain a seventh congressional district in 2002, most likely from Denver's suburbs. Could it be Elway Country?

Elway also became active in community affairs via the Elway Foundation, which he started in 1987. It's raised more than $2 million for the Kempe Center and FACES (Family and Community Education and Support), the education arm of his charities. The money goes to two causes: child abuse and education.

"I got pulled so many different directions doing charity work, I finally said, 'I'd rather have my own foundation where I know where the money's going,'" he said.

"We wanted to keep track and make sure at least 90 percent of the money's going to the charity and not going to work, and that it's going to help and not go to administration fees.

Elway hasn't ruled out a second career in football, either, possibly as an owner. "It intrigues me," he said.

In the meantime, it's the same old routine, routine for John Elway.

At training camp, he stays on the same floor, year after year. In fact, Elway has spent more than one-and-one-quarter years in that Greeley dorm.

"I get off the elevator in the dorm and it's like we never left," he said.

During the season, Elway sits in the same seat on the team plane. Second row from the back. On the aisle.

"When they did change me, whoever sat in my chair, I changed with them," Elway told the *Denver Post* near the end of the 1996 season. "I've been in the same seat for 14 years."

And his days follow a familiar pattern.

On a typical fall morning, he fixes his kids' breakfast, reads the paper, drops off his youngest daughter at school, heads to one of seven auto dealerships he owns, and then to Broncos headquarters. After a long day, it's back to his suburban mansion, and some time with Janet, the kids and the dogs.

When it's time to sleep, Elway flicks on the TV. He can't fall asleep — or remain asleep — without the TV's background flicker. John sleeps with the same pillow he's slept with since he was six years old — the one his mother repairs each time it rips.

"John's an amazing person. He's learned how to handle things. He's become more mature. But it's scary to think what will happen. Sometimes I wish he was a regular guy."

Janet said that in 1983, before John had taken his first NFL center-snap.

Denver coach Dan Reeves admitted he put too much pressure on Elway during his rookie season. "I've got to be more patient," he said. Reeves and Elway agreed after the end of Season One that it had been a mistake not to make Steve DeBerg the starting quarterback.

Chapter 7 —
At War
With Dan Reeves

WHEN THE NEED ARISES, DAN REEVES WILL GO TO fanatical extremes to win a game — especially the tough ones. And the need often arises.

Several years ago, at a nearby country club, the club pro kept bouncing a golf ball on the floor and then catching it on the back of his hand. He bet Reeves $5 he couldn't do it.

Five times Reeves tried it, and five times he fumbled.

Reeves can't think about winning except relentlessly, so it gnawed at him for hours.

"I went home and went out on the patio that night; it was the only place where there was smooth concrete," he said. "It was like 35 degrees out. I practiced and practiced and about froze to death. After about two hours I managed to catch the ball three out of five times.

"The next morning I went to the golf course and asked for the same bet. He said, 'Sure,' and I caught the first one. I got my $5 back."

Not to mention his honor.

"I can't be a loser," Reeves says.

Neither can Elway, which is why he and Reeves were on a collision course from the start. Reeves' determination to succeed against all odds and enemies is just as absolute as Elway's. In fact, their bitter differences over 10 turbulent years stemmed in large part from their fundamental similarities, starting with stubbornness and contempt for defeat and for those unaffected by it.

Not that their differences weren't real.

Elway was the California Golden Boy, blessed with prodigious brilliance and assured of an epic future. Reeves, from the rural South, battled an early illness, battled to get a college scholarship, battled to survive in the NFL as an undrafted free agent, battled to get a foothold as a football coach.

Then he battled with Elway, even though the $5 million quarterback was his meal ticket.

Their star wars often escalated into a Rocky Horror Soap Opera, alternately amusing and embittering fans, who immersed themselves in the high drama and low cunning with a passion normally reserved for family feuds.

"I don't agree with everything John does and he doesn't agree with everything I do," Reeves said, setting a state record for understatement.

The feud was philosophical: Elway wanted a high-tech passing attack; Reeves wanted to play it close to the vest with a running-based scheme. And then, if necessary, turn it over to Elway.

It was personal: Reeves fired Mike Shanahan, Elway's passing guru, not long after Elway had gone public with complaints about Reeves' autocratic ways.

It was messy: Reeves and Elway screamed at one another on the sideline, apologized in the press, bitterly criticized one another in private, then attacked one another in the press.

It was productive: Elway won three AFC Championships under Reeves, as well as enough honors and tributes to fill a lifetime.

And then it was over. After the 1992 season, Reeves was fired, with Elway's prodding. But the embers of their war smoldered.

At his first training camp in the post-Reeves regime, Elway, still white-hot, said: "The last three years have been hell. I know that I would not have been back here if Dan Reeves had been here. It wasn't worth it to me. I didn't enjoy it. It wasn't any fun and I got tired of working with him."

Reeves, in the midst of his first New York Giants training camp, fired back:

"Just tell him it wasn't exactly heaven for me, either. One of these days I hope he grows up. Maybe he'll mature sometime."

Neither Reeves nor Elway had to battle for the hearts and minds of many fans;

they had 'em in their pockets. Elway struggled at first to win over the city. But by his first Super Bowl, he seemed like a fellow who deserved a following.

In 1995, one of his ex-Stanford teammates asked him to play in a golf tournament in Bakersfield, California, to help raise money for one of the local high schools. No problem, Elway said. But a few weeks later, Pat Bowlen hired Shanahan, who promptly scheduled a series of spring mini-camps. Elway called his buddy, and told him he wouldn't be able to attend. Trouble was, he'd papered the neighborhood with flyers and bulletins announcing Elway's appearance. He begged Elway not to back out.

As it turned out, Elway took part in the mini-camp, then flew to Bakersfield on a private plane he had chartered. He missed the golf tournament, but gave a rousing 45-minute speech, donated $1,000 to the school, signed autographs for a couple hours, and then drank beers with his buddy for a couple more kicked-back hours.

Reeves struck fans as a decent man, as well. After a particularly bad defeat at Mile High Stadium, he was driving home on I-25 when he came upon a car that had been plowed from behind by a hit-and-run driver. Reeves and his wife were the first to pull over. A mother and her two children sat in his car while he called Denver police to report the accident. He stayed with the accident victims for 45 minutes until an ambulance arrived, a dutiful Southern gentleman to the end.

The following Sunday, Reeves was on the sideline, wearing steel-rim glasses, and a natty sports jacket, his jaw clenched — probably in anger over his swaggering big-toothed quarterback, who was both his deliverance and despair.

Quarterbacks and their coaches are a notoriously feuding bunch. Their toxic conflicts and anguished entanglements are as inevitable as the next Super Bowl.

In Pittsburgh, Terry Bradshaw and Chuck Noll practically held their noses in contempt around each other. In his rookie season, Bradshaw completed only 38 percent of his passes, led the NFL in interceptions with 24, and threw just six touchdowns. He was fined for being two minutes late for a meeting, and humiliated one Sunday when Noll grabbed him by the shoulders and spun him around like a goofy kid.

It didn't get any better in ensuing years.

During one game, Bradshaw was benched, put back in, and benched again. Fans booed when he went down with an injury — at Bradshaw himself, not the perpetrator. In his fourth season, he lost his starting job to Joe Gilliam and was divorced

Elway wanted to throw more, Reeves wanted to run more, a fundamental difference they could never permanently resolve. Elway grew more disenchanted as he watched other quarterbacks put up big numbers in passing offenses and win as well.

from his wife. Bradshaw, who could not pretend indifference, began leaking spite.

"I'd love to be traded," he said.

Bradshaw and Noll went on to win four Super Bowls, but they continued to snipe at one another long after they'd parted ways. In fact, midway through the 1987 season Bradshaw said Noll should "take a serious, hard look at his future," and that a younger coaching staff was needed. Noll, not surprisingly, never congratulated Bradshaw on making the Hall of Fame.

Quarterback Don Meredith and Dallas coach Tom Landry couldn't get along, either. Landry, baffled by his quarterback's lack of fervor, told him: "Look I don't care whether you like me or not. But I'll crawl on my hands and knees through downtown Dallas to make you respect me."

Meredith was put-off by Landry's robotic ways. When his quarterback retired prematurely, Landry felt he'd personally failed. In 1967, Minnesota quarterback Fran Tarkenton, unable to get along with coach Norm Van Brocklin, asked general manager Jim Finks to be traded. The next day Van Brocklin resigned.

In Dallas, Cowboy coach Barry Switzer almost feared Aikman more than the 49ers. In 1995, the quarterback reportedly grew so disenchanted with Switzer that he planned to meet with Cowboy owners Jerry Jones to discuss Switzer's future. Aikman denied it, but there was history to their mutual ill will. At Oklahoma, Aikman transferred to UCLA after two seasons under Switzer.

Meanwhile, in Boston, coach Bill Parcells and quarterback Drew Bledsoe clawed at one another with undiluted anger. Parcells, a Lombardi disciple, cracked down on his laid-back QB from day one.

"Get away from me," he screamed at Bledsoe late in the 1995 season. "I go and show faith in you, give you a chance to show how you can lead this team, and you screw it up!"

Added Bledsoe: "Sometimes I just want to scream at him, 'Shut up!'"

No one was happier to see Parcells leave for the New York Jets than Bledsoe.

Mike Holmgren and Brett Favre went to war, as well. In 1992, Holmgren staked his future on the cocky rebel party boy, who showed why he deserved that reputation on his first day in Packer Land.

After checking out the Packers' practice facility — which is known as "The Barn"

— Favre spotted Reba McEntire's name on a nearby marquee. McEntire is one of Favre's favorite country musicians, and country music lifts Favre's spirits like nothing else. Favre caught her act that night — all of it — which is why Holmgren was forced to pull aside his new QB after Favre's first mini-camp practice.

"Holmgren asked me what was wrong and if I'd gone out the night before," Favre said. "I told him I had. Coach Holmgren told me, 'Brett, we expect you to be a leader here. We need you to be sharp every day. People are counting on you. Don't let it happen again, OK?'"

Holmgren wanted a disciplined quarterback in the image of Joe Montana to run his precision-based passing attack. Favre — a gambler at heart — wanted to run wild, throw the big strike, make the miracle play. In 1993, he threw 19 TD passes — and an embarrassing 24 interceptions. At one low point, Green Bay fans gave Favre a standing ovation when he prudently tossed the ball out of bounds.

"My question to him in those days was, 'Are you going to be able to control your decision-making or are you going to play every game like it's the Gunfight at the OK Corral?'" Holmgren said. "It was like a big gunslinger type of thing where we were running all over the place and he was throwing all these bombs."

Favre's passion got him into trouble when he became the only quarterback in NFL history to be threatened with a fine from his own team for overzealous celebration.

After a score, Favre would sprint to the end zone and embrace his teammates, often knocking them to the ground. Holmgren was so worried Favre might hurt a teammate, that he told the quarterback he'd be taxed $5,000 the next time.

As late as 1994, Holmgren wasn't sure Favre could be a dependable quarterback, much less a star. When Favre was sidelined with a hip injury that year, he returned to his Kiln, Mississippi home for a week and brooded over his career. By the time he returned, Favre was ready to do it Holmgren's way.

In 1957, the Detroit Lions were confident they could win an NFL title, in large part because of the skill and leadership of quarterback Bobby Layne. In fact, Layne had more influence on the team than its coach, Buddy Parker.

Parker knew it, too. Two nights before the Lions' first exhibition game, the city of Detroit had its annual "Meet the Lions" dinner to launch the team season. At a bar at the back of the room, Layne and his cronies were demonstrating their legendary party style.

The display disgusted Parker, who walked slowly to the microphone when it came time for his customary address to fans. "This team of ours is the worst I've seen in training," he said. "I can't control this group and don't want to get involved in another losing season. I quit, and I'm leaving tonight."

Then Parker left the room, and a stunned audience. But the Lions went on to win their first NFL title, beating Cleveland 59-14 in the championship game.

Reeves didn't want to leave the Broncos. In fact, it was the job of a lifetime, and Reeves had devoted his life to football.

Born and raised in Americus, Georgia, 10 miles from Jimmy Carter's home in Plains, he lived in a world of root beer, letter sweaters and 80-yard runs.

Deacon Dan, as he was known, was an unlikely football hero. He suffered from a slight case of rheumatic fever before he was two, and then came down with a rare kidney ailment. For the next three years he was in and out of hospitals, and few thought he'd ever lead a robust life, much less become a legendary NFL personality.

When he played in his first game, his mother trembled. But hard times only hardened his resolve to succeed in football, a game that transfixed him from the time he first broke a trickle of sweat in a backyard run.

As a kid, he and an older brother would lie awake in their bedroom, with their lights off, grilling one another on tactics. Would you pass or run on third down against this defense or that defense? Would you go for it on fourth and one here or there?

When Reeves' friends went hunting or fishing, Reeves stayed behind, bent over a playbook.

After a splendid high school career, Reeves was recruited by South Carolina — and only South Carolina. After starring in an all-star game, however, the big hitters descended on Reeves, including Alabama and Georgia. But Reeves remained loyal to South Carolina, the school that chose him first.

Reeves became South Carolina's starting quarterback for three years, and good enough, he reasoned, to be drafted by both the NFL and AFL.

He wasn't drafted at all.

Reeves remains a beloved character in Denver, but as the losses mounted, so did angry fans, many of whom wanted to see Elway "turn it loose." Nevertheless, the Broncos won three AFC Championships during the Reeves tenure.

After joining the Dallas Cowboys as a free agent, his future was measured in days. Coach Tom Landry switched Reeves to halfback, then gave him make-or-break pre-season playing time in Birmingham, Alabama. As time ticked away, so did Reeves' hopes.

Then, as his parents watched, Reeves took a pass 67 yards for a touchdown, a running commentary on the role of resolve in the NFL. Following a bone-breaking career, Reeves became a Cowboys assistant coach, and then, surprisingly, a victim of burnout.

"We won Super Bowl (VI) and it was not fun. I had to coach Duane Thomas and I was miserable. He wouldn't talk to anyone, including me. It was terrible. So I quit," Reeves said.

For a year, in an ill-timed career move, Reeves sold townhomes as the North Dallas real-estate boom went south. Although Landry tried to lure him back in mid-season, Reeves' stubbornness and competitiveness precluded an early retirement from the realty business.

When Reeves did return, refreshed and repentant, he was ready for a long run. By the late-'70s, he was a regular on the interview circuit, but head coaching jobs with the New York Giants and Los Angeles Rams passed him by, as did the Auburn University job.

"I thought, 'God, I'm going to be an assistant for the rest of my life.'"

In 1981, Reeves and Mike Ditka, his buddy and confidant, were about to take their first swing on the first hole at a Dallas country club when "The Call" finally came. "The Broncos want to interview you," Landry told him.

Reeves rushed home and into his study, where he worked the phone and his own insights to form a battle plan to convince Broncos owner Edgar Kaiser that he was the best man to steward Denver back to the Super Bowl. It was a waste of time.

"What's your price?" Kaiser asked.

Reeves returned to Dallas to leave it, and create his own legend.

"I barely got a college scholarship. I barely made it to the pros. I tore up my knee in 1968 and I barely got a job as a player-coach. I barely got my job back after the year I quit," he said.

Translation: He'd gone through too much to blow it now.

Reeves left for work at 4 a.m., and returned late at night, driven by a compulsion that left bags under his eyes, and his friends and family members on the sideline of his life.

"He had no flexibility, no real compassion for people at first," said one of his assistants.

In 1981, the Broncos finished with a 10-6 record. Not a bad start for Reeves. But during the strike-shortened 2-7 season in 1982, the Broncos needed a major change — which is where John Elway entered the scene.

As the Broncos brass debated the wisdom of working a deal for the Stanford quarterback, general manager Hein Poulus pulled Reeves aside.

"I was deeply skeptical about Elway's value, and one evening we were having dinner with all the scouts who were in town getting ready for the draft," Poulus said.

"I asked Dan, 'If there was a shot at getting Elway, what would you give up in terms of draft?' He said 'Whatever it takes.'"

Elway and Reeves, however, soon found themselves locked in a state of mutual apprehension and even antipathy. Elway's teammates were equally unsettled by their young coach.

"It was Mutiny on the Bounty," cornerback Louis Wright said. "The players believed Dan was becoming a dictator ... The players were saying, 'Hey, if it's going to be another year of this, then we're going to get Dan out of here. If we have to lose every game, then we're going to lose every game.' The players kept saying 'Somebody had to tell him,' and the players said, 'Louie, you're the player's rep.'"

Wright talked to Reeves, who said he was shocked at hearing himself described as a frosty autocrat.

"He never forgave me," Wright said. "If I'd been a marginal player, I would have been gone the next day."

Instead, Wright retired unexpectedly in the summer of 1987, tired of dealing with Reeves.

Yet from 1984-90, Reeves, along with general manager John Beake, led Denver to three AFC Championships and Super Bowl appearances, won 10 or more games five times — a record unmatched by any team except San Francisco — and possessed a 54-14 home record, tops in the NFL.

And his talent pool was shallow by Super Bowl standards.

Most Super Bowl squads have three or four Hall of Fame candidates. The Broncos had Steve Atwater and Karl Mecklenburg and a couple other Pro Bowlers. But it came down to Elway — and Reeves.

Which is why owner Pat Bowlen gave Reeves a three-year contract extension after the 1988 season. The $3 million deal, good over four seasons, made Reeves the sole commander.

"Nobody has more control over their own destiny than I do," said the beaming coach, who began listing vice-president before coach on his job description.

Added Bowlen: "Having the best coach you can have is every bit as important as having the best quarterback you can possibly have. My philosophy is to pick your guy, give him plenty of rope, and hope he doesn't hang himself."

Reeves worked magic in 1989.

He fired defensive coordinator Joe Collier, a highly regarded tactician, but hired Wade Phillips, who took Denver's D to a new dimension. He drafted safety Steve Atwater, a Pro Bowl regular, and cut starter Mike Harden. He brought back Mike Shanahan, recently fired by Los Angeles Raiders owner Al Davis, to work with Elway.

Then he took the Broncos to the third Super Bowl in four years.

In 1990, however, Reeves' dreams started crumbling.

A few days before a pre-season game at Indianapolis, Reeves experienced a burning sensation in his throat while riding his bike. A minute into a subsequent stress test, a Greeley doctor shut down the machine. Soon Reeves, 46, was loaded into a private jet, pale and barefoot, an intravenous needle in his arm, and shuttled to northern California. There he received an artherectomy, a procedure that slices away plaque obstructing the arteries.

It wasn't literally a heart attack, but it was close enough.

Two years before, Ditka, by then the Bears coach, was benched by a heart attack. That these two rambunctious, combative buddies had serious health problems unnerved their Dallas friends, who still had vivid memories of their unfazed elan.

Reeves grew wary of the close relationship between Elway and Shanahan, suspecting they were scripting plays without his approval. Elway prized Shanahan's input.

True to form, Reeves returned to practice within days. He's a football coach after all and football coaches push themselves to the brink.

For example, Washington coach Joe Gibbs slept in his office at Redskins Park on Monday through Thursday nights, sleep being a short but unwelcome necessity. His wife sent videotapes of their sons to keep him abreast.

John Madden struggled to stay abreast during his Oakland Raiders' coaching days. When his wife informed him their son had to register for a driver's license, the coach said, "How does an 11-year-old qualify for a driver's license?"

"He's 16," she said.

During the strike-shortened 1982 season, work-a-holic Philadelphia Eagle coach Dick Vermeil escaped the football bubble for the first time in eons. "The changing trees, the colors in the field amazed him," wife Carol told *Sports Illustrated.* "I think he thought all fields were green with white stripes on them."

Vermeil later quit, citing burnout.

No one needed to tell John Elway about coaches' stress. He'd watched his dad over the years, and became concerned when Jack left San Jose State for Stanford.

"He was getting up in years and I thought it'd be really tough for him ... and he already had a good job at San Jose State. I just knew how hard it is to win and to compete at Stanford," John said.

Upon his return, Reeves abandoned junk food, even chocolate, his favorite vice. It didn't sweeten his disposition.

Reeves' seething ambition is a force in its own right. So when the Broncos slid to a 5-11 record — and into crises — the 1990 season turned into a wearing voyage for all.

Elway's anxiety and rage had been building for years.

In 1988, in Week Five, he threw down a gauntlet — as well as his helmet — during a 12-0 win over San Diego. The Broncos had failed to produce a touchdown — after penetrating the Chargers' 20 yard line six times — for the first time in 33 games. Never before had Denver won a road game without crossing the goal line.

An infuriated Elway yelled at wide receivers, cursed tight ends, stomped his feet.

"I almost lost it," Elway said.

Added Reeves: "John is the player he is because he's so competitive. He can't let it get to the point where it gets to be a problem."

Elway had nine interceptions and three touchdown passes at the time. It got worse.

"He's just tired. He got tired of losing the Super Bowl and having to face all the second-guessers," Terry Bradshaw said. "He didn't play that poorly (in the Super Bowl). He did all right, but they lost. It drains you. It exhausts you. You scratch your head and wear yourself out. The Broncos needed a year off."

Elway's primary problem remained Reeves' conservative offense, and his unwillingness to alter it. "Why should I?" Reeves told himself.

No one was more conservative than Giants coach Bill Parcells, whose two Super Bowl wins were unembarrasable proof of the wisdom of the old nostrums.

"We'd be up 14-3 in the second quarter, and he'd give me the kill-the-clock sign," New York quarterback Phil Simms told *Sports Illustrated*. "He'd point his index finger like a gun at his watch. I'd run the 45-second clock down to one and just milk the clock."

Ironically, only a decade before, Reeves had been regarded as the creative mind behind the Cowboys' cosmopolitan offense. Even as a player, Reeves used his head. During the 1967 Ice Bowl game against Green Bay, Reeves, a halfback, suggested a halfback option pass to quarterback Don Meredith. A while later, Reeves hit Lance Renztel on a 50-yards TD strike, lifting Dallas to a 17-14 lead. Green Bay won the NFL title, but Reeves won Landry's enduring respect.

In 1990, however, Reeves seemed rigid, unimaginative, staid — especially to Elway, who knew the times were changing.

During the '70s and '80s, Buddy Ryan, a Minnesota and Chicago assistant, developed a guerrilla defense that was sweeping the league. Blitzing was a staple of the game, but Ryan took it to a new lethal level. Lawrence Taylor, Wilber Marshall, Andre Tippitt and other large mobile headhunters were willing to risk serious injury for "kill shots." Enfeebled quarterbacks were fast becoming an endangered species.

In a shrewd counter-attack, San Francisco coach Bill Walsh perfected an attack

— the West Coast — which employed an uncommonly high number of receivers from sideline to sideline, enabling a quarterback to throw shorter, smarter passes that short-circuited speed rushers.

Only once during the Reeves regime had Elway thrown as many as 20 touchdowns in a season. Routine quarterbacks routinely did that. He had never surpassed 4,000 yards, and never averaged more than two 300-games per year.

A Hall of Fame official, speaking off the record, told a Broncos official that it would be "a shame for posterity's sake if John Elway never had the chance to play for a team that emphasized passing."

As the '80s gave way to the '90s, Elway gave up on making the Hall of Fame.

"We rarely threw except on passing downs, and people knew when we were going to throw," Elway said later. "That was the style of the offense. We didn't have the quick game we have now. When people were coming at us, we weren't able to get out of there. If we had a tough time protecting on that day, it usually made for a long day.

"We had some good years. We had a good offensive team, but it seemed to go downhill. You look at (Reeves') offense now the last three or four years (with the New York Giants), and it's been dead last in the league. He hasn't moved with the game.

"Dan's been in the same system ever since he's been (in the NFL). If I hadn't stepped up to a better system, who knows where my numbers would've been?"

In 1993, after 10 years of worn-out arguments and piercing protests, Elway detonated a bomb when he told a *Denver Post* columnist that players considered Reeves aloof, autocratic, inflexible.

"This year has been the worst," said Elway, ostensibly representing the team. "We hardly talk to each other unless it's game time. I think I'm going to have to express my opinions ... I'm going to have to go to Dan.

"They might not like what I have to say, but I'm going to give it to them and they can take it for what it's worth. I don't care if you use the part about more friction between Dan and me. If he wants to confront me about it, it's probably better anyway. Because if I don't do it now, I'll do it at the end of

Owner Pat Bowlen and coach Dan Reeves had a long run, but after the
1992 season, Bowlen was convinced the Broncos needed to head in a
different direction. He fired Reeves and replaced him with Wade Phillips.

the year anyway."

Elway's remarks were a rip to Reeves' heart.

"I was totally blind-sided," he said. "I didn't see anything wrong."

After the shock abated, Reeves became furious that Elway had gone public with his complaints instead of meeting privately with him.

"They were both very accomplished, very talented, very confident about what they're doing and the way they're doing it," Denver fullback Reggie Rivers said. "I'm sure that contributed to the fact they clashed heads. They both believed so strongly that the way they were doing things was the right way."

At that point, Bowlen had to step in and enforce a wobbly detente.

"I'm not a politician," Elway said. "Politicians always make everything fuzzy, but I can't do that. Sometimes with the media, you've got to cover things up ... But I like to let people know where I'm coming from."

At the time of his latest declaration, three of the Broncos' six defeats had turned on interceptions Elway had thrown — including two against both Cleveland and San Diego. A prankster, tired of what he perceived as Elway's whining, placed a baby bib over Elway's caricature on a billboard.

But many players sided with Elway.

"It's a crime," linebacker Karl Mecklenburg said. "We grind it out, and every once in a while John would get to do something spectacular in the last two minutes."

After Elway's public criticism, however, Reeves gave his quarterback the input he craved. The following season, Elway expanded his control, even participating in Tuesday strategy sessions. But as the season progressed, Elway's role diminished.

Reeves added wrinkles to the game plan with each passing week, eventually over-loading the QB with minutia. In time, Elway was forced to record plays on a wrist-band cheat sheet.

Eventually, Reeves regained almost total control of play-calling. By season's end, he was sending in plays almost exclusively, much as before.

The Broncos made it to the AFC Championship, where a 10-7 loss to Buffalo kept Reeves and Elway from another shot at Super Bowl redemption.

Within months, they were taking shots at one another. During the off-season, Elway presented Reeves with a wish-list: offensive linemen, and big-play receiver(s). That angered Elway's offensive linemen, and perhaps Reeves, who proceeded to select UCLA quarterback Tommy Maddox rather than Tennessee wide receiver Carl Pickens with a first-round pick. That was doubly humiliating to Elway: not only had Reeves ignored his request, he had actually picked a quarterback — Elway's heir apparent — and then publicly discussed the post-Elway era.

Elway sagged.

"I'm starting to feel old," he said. "I didn't think 31 was old, but now I'm really starting to feel old with the talk of passing the torch. I just saw a twinkle at the end of the tunnel. I think it opened up a little bit."

The troubles didn't end there. In another move that hurt and humiliated Elway, Reeves fired Shanahan, who was not only Elway's confidant and long-time friend, but his link to the passing game, as well.

In 1991, Reeves even discussed a trade with Washington coach Joe Gibbs that would have sent Elway to the Redskins. Reeves insisted Gibbs had broached the idea.

"I was aware that there had been some discussions between Gibbs and Dan," Bowlen told *Denver Post* reporter Adam Schefter in 1996. "I just said, 'There's no way we're going to do the deal. Forget it.' So it never got off the talking-on-the-telephone stage."

Elway, however, believes the talks were serious. Following the 1991 season, he spoke with former Washington running back Earnest Byner, who informed him of the details.

"(Byner) said, 'I thought you were going to be a Redskin,'" Elway said. "I said, 'What are you talking about?' So I got him to tell me the whole story. When I heard about it, it didn't surprise me because Dan was still here."

Elway contacted his agent, who, after making some calls, verified the story.

In 1992, the final phase began. Reeves and Elway are the rarest of that rare species who consider any defeat unpalatable, any time.

In 1985, during the AFC West coaches' meeting, Reeves was beating all comers with his standard trick: in three tries, he could blow a dime from a table into a water glass. In fact, he could do it with a quarter.

"In preparation, I had brought a few half dollars with me," former Broncos beat writer T.J. Simers recalled. "I knew Reeves was so competitive that he couldn't turn down a challenge. I figured he'd come around."

Simers and Dave Krieger, another *News* beat writer, allowed Reeves to try the half-dollar trick with a butter dish for a lower trajectory, but the two sides argued whether the butter pats should stay in the dish. They couldn't agree.

When the reporters returned to the hotel, Reeves was in a crouch, his eyes level with a table-top, working on the latest trick.

"You still want to do it?" he asked.

"Sure," they answered.

Reeves failed in three tries.

"Now Reeves is irritated," Simers said. "He starts walking around the lobby, running his hand over every surface. Eventually, he called us to his room. He goes into the bathroom, and finally blows the half-dollar into the glass on the sink. This wasn't for money. He just had to prove he could do it."

Think Elway doesn't think that way? Ask anyone who's played him in, say, gin.

"We play gin all the time," Broncos assistant coach Gary Kubiak told Mickey Herskowitz in his book *The Quarterbacks*. "He'll be killing me, winning game after game, and then I might finally win a hand and John throws the danged cards against the wall. There's a competitive streak in everything he does.

"The thing that's interesting to me is watching him change ... On Saturday, he is one person. Then Sunday, well, the change is like night and day. On game day the butterflies are jumping in him and it's time to play football. Usually he is this pleasant, outgoing guy. Then, all of a sudden, it's like he cuts it off and a curtain drops. We might start looking at football tapes on a Sunday morning and the conversation just stops."

In an ironic twist, Reeves finally went down when Elway went down. On what seemed like a routine hit, on a 9-yard run during a 27-13 win over the New York Giants, Elway bruised a tendon in his right shoulder. At the time, the Broncos had a 7-3 record, and appeared on track for another playoff run. But Elway missed the next four games, and neither Tommy Maddox nor Shawn

Moore could salvage a single victory. In fact, their inept play made it clear the Broncos, who finished with an 8-8 record, were a one-man band.

"It became obvious to me that we had a situation where if we lost our quarterback, our franchise player, we would have trouble beating anybody," Bowlen said. "I had that feeling all along, but the injury certainly confirmed that. Probably somewhere in the back of my head was the idea that John has maybe four or five seasons left and we had to give him the opportunity to win the big one. I felt that our offense had become so predictable through the nine or 10 years that sometimes our opponents knew exactly what we were doing before we did."

But Bowlen had another reason to fire Reeves. As the cost and risk of running a franchise increased in the '90s, owners throughout the league wanted more control of their investments. He thought Reeves had excessive control.

Furthermore, Bowlen simply wanted to start over.

Major-league baseball was coming, and neither Denver, nor the Broncos' unrivaled hold on the city, would be the same. Reeves was a celebrity sacrifice, one final attempt to hold onto a passing time and place.

Nonetheless, Reeves was graceful to the end.

"I know I have a tremendous respect for John Elway. I've always said that. But I'm not sure that's a mutual feeling," he said in his final press conference.

The Chicago Bears' Ditka spoke on Reeves' behalf, singling out Elway for condemnation — and culpability.

"(Bowlen's) letting the inmates run the asylum," he said. "Ask other coaches what a magnificent job Dan Reeves has done. I don't think John Elway became John Elway for any other reason that Dan Reeves was the head coach. Dan Reeves developed him and helped him. Dan Reeves is the reason the Broncos went to three Super Bowls. I don't care who owns, who kicks, who quarterbacks. Do I make my point?"

Elway insisted he had no input on the Reeves' question. *News* columnist Bob Kravitz wrote: "Sorry, not buying it. Elway did have input and should have had input. He is the most important player on the team; it's disingenuous for him to suggest he has had no more say than, for instance, Brad Daluigo, in Reeves' future.

"Is he afraid of being cast in the same light as Magic Johnson, who presided over

Elway can usually be found in the center of the action, but during a 13-10 loss to San Diego in 1993 he felt like a spectator.

Reeves made a graceful exit - seen here with owner Pat Bowlen - during his farewell press conference. His final record in Denver was 117-79-1.

Paul Westhead's demise, or Randall Cunningham, who helped usher out Buddy Ryan?"

Bowlen stepped in to defend his quarterback.

"John has had some things to say in the past in the heat of the moment," Bowlen said. "But John's a player, not a coach, and players don't make decisions on who coaches.

"John didn't have any influence on the decision, and I don't believe he'd want to have any."

Later, Bowlen said, "Certainly (Reeves') relationship with John wasn't the greatest, and I think it's fair to say John's future here was in question if Dan had stayed. But that wasn't the biggest reason I fired him. It was just the sense we had gone as far as we were going to go."

With Reeves gone, Elway preferred to remain in Denver, though he could have become an unrivaled, unrestricted free agent when his contract expired following the 1993 season.

"I don't want to go anywhere else," he said. "The money isn't the big thing. I think, if you really want to move, that's what would make you do it, and I'm not interested. It's a lot more important for me to stay here, for my family and those types of things, than it is to go somewhere else and make a little more money."

In 1996, Elway and Jeff Hostetler chatted on the Internet in preparation for a Monday night game. Reeves was on their minds, even in Cyberspace. "Preparing for you this weekend, our defense has decided to bring in Dan Reeves as a consultant," said Hostelter, who didn't re-sign with the Giants after Reeves became their coach in '93. "We figure he did such a good job of holding you down before, he could do it again."

What would have happened if Elway had stayed healthy in 1992, the Broncos finished 13-3, and then made another Super Bowl run? Bowlen later admitted he'd have probably given Reeves a new contract, one that probably would have extended for the remainder of the Elway years.

Coach Wade Phillips hired Jim Fassel as his offensive coordinator. Fassel had coached Elway at Stanford, and was considered an expert in the passing game. "I've always said Jim Fassel was responsible for getting me to this point," Elway said.

Chapter 8 —
The Lost Years

FOR TOO MANY YEARS, JOHN ELWAY HAD ARRIVED AT
training camp with a look of foregone disillusion. After checking into his dorm
room, Elway would report to practice, and his doleful duties, and another season
would open about as pleasantly as a wound.

But in 1993, the care-worn, 33-year-old quarterback felt as unencumbered as a
freshman at the University of Northern Colorado campus. Nearly everyone did.

"The best way I can describe Wade Phillips is that people just want to be around
him," linebacker Karl Mecklenburg said of the Broncos' new head coach. "Dan
Reeves' way is the way of the past. Atmosphere matters."

Welcome to Wade World, and a kinder, gentler NFL.

Elway welcomed it, gratefully.

"Is it different?" he asked. "Well, for one thing it wasn't much of a day at camp
last year if there weren't at least five or six fights. There's none of that intimida-
tion … tension … fear."

Instead, there was a new way of doing things in every area, especially on offense,
where Elway went back to his roots.

The West Coast scheme had gone national in the '80s and '90s, to Green Bay
and Philadelphia and Kansas City and Minnesota, and now, to Denver, which
had been flyover country during all of Elway's tenure, now entering its second
decade.

While Reeves was leaving the Broncos to become head coach of the New York
Giants, Jim Fassel was leaving the Giants, where he'd been an assistant, to
become the Broncos' offensive coordinator.

Elway began anew in 1993 under head coach Wade Phillips, who opened up the offense and new opportunities for No. 7 and receivers such as Jerry Evans, shown here. But the excitement of the first days began to fade as losses mounted. The Broncos finished with a 9-7 record, which is nothing to get excited about in Denver.

It was a perfect swap for Elway, who was eager to rack up some big numbers, especially for a West Coast man. Fassel had recruited Elway to Stanford, where he helped him set five NCAA passing records.

"I've always said Jim Fassel was responsible for getting me to this point," he said. "He improved my technique, taught me fundamentals, and put me in an offense where I could thrive."

Critics said Elway wasn't a good "touch" passer, and therefore was unsuited for the West Coast scheme.

In fact, many regarded Elway as a brawny he-man who raced from sideline-to-sideline in the final seconds trying to save the day with one final heave.

Nothing irked Elway more. Fassel had been an assistant to Bill Walsh at Stanford, so Elway had employed many of the system's schemes during his spangled college career.

In fact, in Elway's nirvana he — not Joe Montana — would have quarterbacked the 49ers during their dynastic days. He had the arm, background and training to be chief wizard for Walsh's wonderful high-tech machine. He was sure of it, as was Phillips.

"If we had Earl Campbell instead of John Elway, like we did at Houston, we'd be running the ball straight ahead and over people," Phillips said. "But when you have a quarterback as talented as Elway, you start to think what you can do to take advantage of his skills. I didn't want the run-and-shoot, because you sacrifice options. So that leaves the Walsh system. Spread the ball around. Use passes to control the ball. Let John throw."

Before he mastered it, Elway had to re-learn it, so for the first time in a decade he burned the midnight oil over a playbook. He also had to make some major adjustments on the field, where he'd developed a savior complex during his Broncos years, Fassel said.

"He's going to have to learn that he doesn't need to press anymore," he said. "When he does, when he tries to do everything, I believe he doesn't perform up to his capabilities. His greatness will come out of his natural reactions to each play … To gain 40 yards on a pass play, that doesn't mean you always have to throw the ball 40 yards."

Shannon Sharpe was just a seventh-round draft choice in 1990, but within three years he was a Pro-Bowl regular and Elway's go-to man. He led the Broncos in receptions in 1993 with 81, third-best in the AFC.

Let the receivers do some of the work, Fassel urged, and then sit back and enjoy the ride, *ala* Montana.

"An offense is about getting guys in open spaces and open areas, and that's what the West Coast is all about," says former Los Angeles Rams quarterback Pat Haden. "For years and years, people never made you defend (the width of the field). Everyone always defended you vertically, but not horizontally. This offense has made people do it horizontally. It's changed the nature of the game.

"In fact, these days the game has changed to the point that the greatest athletes are probably now at wide receiver rather than running back. You rarely see long runs anymore in the NFL — a long run is 15 yards. Today, wide receivers are to a wide extent glorified running backs in the sense that you get them the ball at five yards and then hope they can go 60. You throw quick passes and let the wide receiver/running backs make long runs."

Sid Gillman sensed as much decades ago. Over the years, the eighty-something passing guru has designed offenses for seven teams in the NFL, AFL and USFL. But Gillman began experimenting with multiple-set alignments and passing concepts as an assistant at Dennison College in Greenville, Ohio, where he was head coach from 1944-47.

As head coach of the University of Cincinnati from 1949 to '54, Gillman continued to develop his air attack, though it was considered effete — even effeminate — by football's fundamentalists, who were fanatically grounded in the power running game.

Gillman used the Los Angeles Rams and the L.A. Coliseum as a staging ground for his aerial schemes. In 1955 his team won the NFL's Western Conference championship with the revolutionary passing game, which moved at express speed through conventional defenses. Ninety thousand fans, including Hollywood's elite, routinely filled the Coliseum, which seemed like the NFL's version of Tommorowland.

His mantra was simple: Spread the field. Place wide receivers on the far edges to cover more ground and open more holes. Fill all the passing lanes. Read the defense. Hit the receiver on the break. Use all eligible receivers on all plays. Use backs and tight ends as main receivers most of the time.

After five seasons with the Rams, Gillman moved to the AFL's Los Angeles Chargers, who soon moved to San Diego. With quarterback John Hadl, wide receiver Lance Alworth and running back Keith Lincoln, the Chargers won five divisional championships during their first six years, and won the 1963 AFL Championship.

In those early NFL days, Gillman's brainy space-age ball lured many converts, including Al Davis, then a Chargers' assistant. Gillman was the ultimate X's and O's technocrat, even on his weekly television show. In 1966, as he was explaining the mechanics of a slant pattern in minute, monotonous detail, an Oakland Raiders' assistant coach watched in rapt silence in his San Diego hotel room.

It was a revelation for Bill Walsh, who ruminated about Gillman's passing principles in the ensuing years. During his first stint at Stanford in the late '70s, Walsh took those precepts, and then refined them into the West Coast scheme he made famous with the 49ers.

Because it's designed for low-risk, high-volume production, quarterbacks who run the West Coast offense are the envy of those who don't.

"Sometimes you watch Steve Young, and you don't see him hit the ground all day," Chicago Bears quarterback Rick Mirer said. "It's a lot easier than taking a beating. The thing I like most is that there's a lot of high-percentage passing. It's not really risky. It's not a matter of having to throw 20 (yards)-and-outs all day."

Added New York Jets quarterback Neil O'Donnell: "Those defensive linemen and linebackers are faster than ever. With quick passes, you can protect the quarterbacks from them."

Elway embraced the new offense with open arms, much as his receivers, who stood to gain as much — especially yardage.

The summer of '93 was significant for another reason: free agency had been loosed on the NFL, meaning an owner could re-shape his team overnight. The Broncos signed Minnesota Vikings linemen Brian Habib and Gary Zimmerman, as well as Rod Bernstine, a large, pass-catching fullback late of the Chargers. Prior to that season, Elway had never played with a Pro Bowl receiver, and he'd been protected by only one Pro Bowl offensive lineman, guard Keith Bishop.

As the season approached, Phillips' laid-back ways impressed newcomers and old-timers alike. Under the autocratic, frosty Reeves, players were required to follow an extensive array of edicts, which Phillips promptly scrapped.

"It takes a bit to get an old guy like me excited," veteran safety Dennis Smith said. "But the attitude's looser. In the past, when I didn't dress for practice, I'd have to come out with my helmet. Ridiculous. It was Dan doing things to be doing things. But now it's different. Everybody feels part of the team. Everybody's excited."

On opening day, Elway used nine receivers against the New York Jets during a 26-20 victory at Mile High Stadium, and at least six in every ensuing game. That was only the start. He produced 394 yards of total offense against Green Bay; completed 13 straight passes against Minnesota and 10 in a row against Seattle; threw for more than 300 yards in three games, including 361 in the regular-season finale against the Raiders; completed over 60 percent of his passes in 11 of 16 games; and was named AFC Offensive Player of the Week twice.

At season's end, Elway ranked first in the AFC in quarterback rating (92.8), passing attempts (551), completions (348), touchdown passes (25) and passing yards (4,030). He was named the AFC's Most Valuable Player and was the conference's starter for the Pro Bowl. But no one was pleased with the results. The Broncos might have finished third in the NFL in points, but they had a 9-7 record, one game better than the Reeves-led team the year before that had played without Elway for four games.

And when the Broncos ended their season with back-to-back losses against the Raiders (33-30 in the regular-season finale and 42-24 in the playoffs), the stats and honors seemed frivolous, even irrelevant. Elway was receiving as much pity as praise.

It was obvious what must be done. The Raiders' Jeff Hostetler had passed for 604 yards and six touchdowns in the final two games. As he lofted one bomb after another during the playoff romp, Denver defensive coordinator Charlie Waters sat on the bench, his head resting in his hands.

"We need some defensive help," Phillips said. "That should be clear to anybody."

But instead of acquiring some, the Broncos signed free-agent wide receiver

Elway and the Broncos were always primed for the Raiders. But in 1994 they were blown away by their bitter rivals 48-16 at Mile High Stadium. Fans booed Phillips, and the Broncos, who lost their Mile High Mystique that day.

Anthony Miller (formerly of San Diego), and then traded for receiver and local favorite Mike Pritchard, the former Falcon who played at the University of Colorado and who ranked fifth on the all-time NFL list for most catches in the first three seasons of a career.

"Three points more a game last year, and we would have been 14-2," said Phillips, explaining the emphasis on offense.

The Broncos opened Year Two of the Phillips' era at home against San Diego. They jumped to a 24-7 lead, with Elway throwing a 50-yard TD to Mike Pritchard, and an 8-yard scoring pass to Glyn Milburn. But the Chargers surged back early in the second period, moving 83 yards on four plays, culminating with Stan Humphries' 47-yard scoring bomb to Shawn Jefferson.

Elway tossed an interception just two plays into the Broncos' next possession, setting up the Chargers at the Broncos' 41. Four plays later, Humphries connected with wide receiver Mark Seay for a 29-yard score. For the second consecutive time, they failed to convert the two-point conversion, but the Chargers had nonetheless cut the deficit to 24-19.

After a punt by both teams, the Broncos moved from their 28 to San Diego's 5, facing third and one. Elway was picked off by safety Stanley Richard at the Charger 1-yard line. He returned it 99 yards for a touchdown. After converting the two-point conversion, the Chargers led 27-24.

The second half was just as wild and erratic. With 4:01 left, Natrone Means' 1-yard scoring run lifted the Chargers to a 37-34 lead. After taking possession at their own 25, the Broncos drove to the Chargers 3 with just 43 seconds remaining. On second down, Elway rolled right and spotted a wide-open Anthony Miller in the end zone. As he started to throw his game-winning TD, however, the ball slipped from Elway's grasp.

Chargers' linebacker Junior Seau caught the fumble before it hit the ground.

From that point, the Chargers were bound for the Super Bowl, and the Broncos for catastrophe. The following week, the Broncos dropped a 25-22 overtime decision to the New York Jets. During Game Three, a capacity crowd at Mile High Stadium saw the Los Angeles Raiders score touchdowns on their first four possessions, with drives of 58, 69, 61 and 35 yards.

It got worse. The Raiders continued to score at will — on a field where shutouts had once been considered a Bronco rite of nature — en route to a 48-16 win.

By game's end, Broncos fans had turned on the team. For years, Mile High Stadium had been the NFL's version of Shangri-La. Every non-strike game had been sold out since 1970. The Broncos had the best home record since 1977.

But the Mile High Mystique vaporized that day, even in the South Stands.

The South Stands are not Perrier Country. Blue-collared fans with hot-button passion respond en masse to transgressions against the Bronco way. Hank Stram knew as much in 1966. As his Kansas City Chiefs built an overwhelming lead, he knew South Standers were building an overpowering ire to punish his men. With that in mind, he ordered an onside kick in the final minutes. Then he ordered his captain to tell the Broncos it was coming. In other words, Stram wanted the Broncos to fall on the ball, and then mercifully kill the clock. The Broncos couldn't even do that. The Chiefs recovered, and scored again, giving them a 56-10 win.

To get to their locker room, the Chiefs had to pass under the South Stands. Stram ordered his players to put on their helmets and to arm themselves with makeshift shields. They needed them. As they neared their locker room, the Chiefs were inundated with a missile shower.

Dan Reeves induced the wrath of South Standers in 1990. During the final game of a 5-11 season, Reeves didn't allow Sammy Winder to finish his career with a TD.

"That's chicken ....," a fan screamed.

"I'll meet you any day," Reeves screamed back as two assistants pulled him away from trouble and into the locker room.

Reeves was still seething when he met the press.

"Nobody's going to challenge how tough I am," he said.

In 1994, it was Phillips' turn for a verbal caning. As he walked toward the Broncos' locker room, the venom poured from above.

"Get him out of here," one fan yelled to Bowlen.

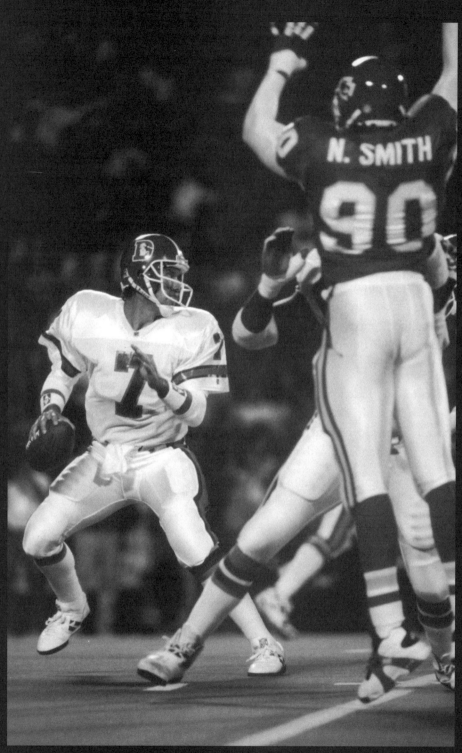

No man sacked Elway more than Kansas City's Neil Smith, one of the league's quickest pass rushers. No Bronco was happier to see Smith join the Bronco's in 1997 than Elway.

Bowlen did, at the end of the season. But before he did, Mile High Stadium went silent.

"During some of the losses at Mile High, it was as quiet as I've ever heard it," said ex-Broncos safety Billy Thompson, now the team's director of player relations. "That really bothered me because it was something I wasn't used to. I knew something was wrong. I wanted to say something, to start a fight, just to shake things up."

The Broncos finished 7-9 during Phillips' final season, giving the team a 24-25 record from 1992-94. Even worse, the Broncos lost seven home games, including 17-10 to lowly Tampa Bay in 1993, and 30-28 to New Orleans in the 1994 season-finale, where there were 10,781 no-shows despite pleasant 60-degree weather. The Broncos finished with a 4-4 home record.

But the ultimate insult was the Raiders' romp.

"The game was clearly one of the low points in Broncos history," Saccomano said. "You're playing your fiercest rival, with all the classic elements in play, you're 0-2 and you desperately need a win. And then you're not ready to play? Why not?"

Added Elway: "The one thing we really had going for us back in the '80s was the home-field advantage. We lost it in the Raiders' game."

Losing the home-field advantage was not the only killer blow to the Broncos' mystique.

A lack of intensity — and resolve — haunted Phillips' team when it mattered most. The Broncos had a record of 2-9 in games decided by three or fewer points and 3-4 in crucial December games.

After a 42-19 loss to the San Francisco 49ers on December 17, which ended Denver's 1994 playoff hopes, Shannon Sharpe openly questioned the team's will to win. "Sometimes I wonder," he said, "is everybody giving everything they've got?"

When Phillips finally lost his temper during another listless practice, his players welcomed the outburst, figuring it was long overdue.

"Some of the guys thought he lacked the control you needed as a head coach," Broncos linebacker Elijah Alexander said. "I think that was the biggest thing. Pat Bowlen thought that, and a lot of people around the organization felt that way. And I think that might have been his biggest downfall."

"I was down, really down, those two years," All-Pro safety Steve Atwater said. "I'd come home in a bad mood. I was sick of it. It wasn't like playing football. It was like going to work. I was ready to leave Denver."

Elway wasn't faring much better. As the losses mounted — 27-20 to Buffalo, 31-28 to Kansas City, 27-21 to the Los Angeles Rams, 42-19 to San Francisco — so did his sense of futility.

"Wins and losses are always what it's all about," he said. "Especially when you go into a game you think you should win. It makes them hurt that much more."

Growing old in the NFL is almost too much to endure, even for a durable icon like Elway, who'd undergone countless surgeries, and been sacked more than anyone except Fran Tarkenton.

But Elway's pain was not physical. It was emotional, no small fact for a man who had always played with breath-taking verve.

"Sometimes you'd like to shoot him with a tranquilizer gun," Reeves said in 1986. "He gets so pumped up, sometimes it takes him a while to settle down."

During his third season, after an interception, Elway fought off two blockers and made a touchdown-saving tackle. "I figure if I can give seven points or save seven points, I will," he said.

But now, some wondered if Elway was on the verge of burnout.

"If you were going to graph Elway's skill level, I imagine he'd be one of those guys who go immediately to the 95 percentile level," former Raiders linebacker Matt Millen said. "Then it would be a straight line across the graph — at 95 percent — and then in year 15 it finally drops off. Not a gradual drop-off. He's going to be one of those guys who all of a sudden really drops off. But I'd venture to say that the thing that causes a breakdown in his production will not be physical. It'll be in his head.

"You start to lose interest. I remember in my final year, I was thinking, 'I know I can do all these things, but why? What for? There is no more to prove, no one left to prove it to.' If you're Elway, you can say. '(I) want to be All-Pro — except I've been All-Pro. I want to be in big games — except I've been in big games. I want to be one of the best — except I am one of the best now.'

"It's like you've exhausted all your reasons for playing."

Elway remained obsessed about winning the Super Bowl. When Reeves departed, and the Broncos used the free-agent market to replenish their offense, he felt another Super Bowl was inevitable, even imminent.

But by 1994, Elway knew how hard it is to get back to the mountain-top, something Anthony Munoz had experienced in 1991, during his 11th season with the Cincinnati Bengals.

"We'd gone to the Super Bowl in '89, we'd won the AFC Central in '90, and then all of a sudden in '91 and '92 we're going 5-11 and 3-13," he said.

"You start wondering, 'How many years is it going to take to turn this around? Is this really going to pay off? Do we really have a chance to get back to the playoffs, much less the Super Bowl?' It starts working on your mind. It starts taking an emotional toll, more than any physical stress."

When the Cincinnati Bengals started losing, Munoz started viewing his surroundings with a new perspective, especially younger ones.

"Guys started coming in who were in elementary school when I had started my NFL career," Munoz said. "Their interests were different, the things we did were different, everything was different."

Elway got a sense of that in 1992, when rookie center Bob Meeks turned to him and said, "Excuse, me, sir, Mr. Elway, but what was the snap count?"

And when New England quarterback Drew Bledsoe said: "I was in fifth grade when Elway and Marino were drafted."

With each passing season, Elway had less and less in common with his younger teammates, some of whom were grade-school students when he'd first burst on the national scene. They talked gangsta'rap, he talked Springsteen. They loved

For a while, Elway was all smiles during the Phillips era. At the end of
the 1993 season, he ranked first in the AFC in quarterback rating and
was the AFC's Most Valuable Player. Nevertheless, Denver finished 9-7,
which pleased no one.

locker room hi-jinx; he kept to himself in a corner locker. "He doesn't even know what they're talking about," a ballboy said.

"When I quit, I was lucky, because I just walked away," said ex-49ers Randy Cross. "But that's exactly why I quit. The game was not fun anymore. The way you're treated is pretty sophomoric, as far as being in bed by 11:15 and all the other little things. As much fun as it is, it's a tradeoff."

Los Angeles Rams quarterback Pat Haden had exhausted all his reasons for playing when he threw in the towel. He'd been a hometown hero at Southern Cal, so he was living a dream when he joined the Rams in 1976.

In the second game of the 1976 season he guided the Rams to a 10-10 tie against Minnesota, outplaying Fran Tarkenton. As a result, he was tossed into a whirling quarterback controversy. He battled James Harris and Ron Jaworski for the No. 1 spot.

By the next season the Rams had traded Harris to San Diego and Jaworski to Philadelphia. They added Joe Namath and rookie Vince Ferragamo. Namath won the starting job, but quickly gave way to Haden.

Two years later, Haden broke a finger on his passing hand, which allowed Ferragamo to lead the Rams into Super Bowl XIV. Haden won the job in preseason the following year, but was sidelined for the season following an injury in the opener.

Eventually, Haden realized the spark of compulsion was missing from his game.

"I was just drained," he said. "It was emotional fatigue. The constant second-guessing and criticism after our playoff losses just wore me down, mentally. Even when you try not to listen to it or read it, someone says, 'Hey, did you hear what so-and-so said about you?' At that point, I just wanted to do something else with my life."

Haden said Elway faced even more pressure in Denver.

"For Elway, it would be very, very difficult to wake up every Sunday morning and say, 'For us to win, I have to play great — not good — but great. He's been in that situation virtually every Sunday in his career.

"And I don't think there's any one person more identified with a single team than John Elway is with Denver. It's another big burden."

Many quarterbacks flourish in old age. Staubach started his NFL career four years late because of a Navy commitment, didn't win the starting job until his third season, missed most of the 1973 season with an injury, and didn't have his first 300-yard game until his 72nd NFL game. Early in his NFL career, one of Staubach's Dallas teammates said: "If he called his own plays, he'd throw 65 passes a game, 80 percent to a double-covered receiver." That wasn't his only problem.

But when he retired in 1979, he was the highest-ranked quarterback of all time.

Len Dawson's NFL career began in 1957 when the Pittsburgh Steelers made him a first-round draft pick. But in five forgettable seasons, he threw only 45 passes. In 1962, he jumped to the AFL's Dallas Texans from sheer frustration.

Dawson retired in 1975, after winning four AFL passing titles and leading the Chiefs to three championships, including a win in the 1970 Super Bowl. His 19-year career was longer than any quarterback's except George Blanda's.

Ken Stabler's long, trying apprenticeship paid off in the long run, as well. In the Sugar Bowl, his final game for Alabama, Stabler blew out a knee. Oakland picked him in the second round of the 1968 draft, but Stabler spent the entire season rehabilitating his knee. In 1969, he abruptly left camp, convinced coach John Madden was ignoring him. Stabler returned in 1970 and hung around for three more empty seasons. By 1973, Stabler could take no more. But his fortunes changed. He led the Raiders into five conference title games and was named the AFC Player of the Year in '74 and '76.

In 1995, Elway was 35, and the glory days of AFC Championships seemed an impossible distance away. It would take a new coach to breathe new life into Elway. It would take a new coach to make the game fun again.

It would take Mike Shanahan, reasoned Bowlen.

"I knew, after a very short time, that the combination of Wade and myself just wasn't going to cut it ..." Bowlen said. "I really didn't intend to get that involved, but it was a whole new world for Wade and me both. Plus we had the new system, the salary cap, free agency. We sort of depended on each other, feeling our way along in the dark. We were like kids in a candy store (with free agency). We didn't pay much attention to specific positions where we needed help, and character wasn't as much an issue as it needed to be."

When Bowlen hired Shanahan, he fired up Elway.

"When it comes to game time, you still want to go out and compete," he said. "I want to have fun and that's the real fun — the game. As time goes on, you really lose the enthusiasm for the practice and the off-season work and the things it takes to get ready for a season, like the meetings. All those things really start to drag you down in a hurry. But I don't think I'll ever really lose my competitive desire, my desire to play.

"Winning the Super Bowl is the number one thing. We've never won one, and we've been there three times. You'd like to be known as being able to win the Big One."

Elway wasn't in peak form during a 24-19 win over Oakland in Denver in Week 15 of the 1996 season. He threw for 206 yards and for one TD, and was intercepted once. But it was his 126th win as a starter, an NFL record. Shanahan gave him the game ball afterward.

Chapter 9 —
The West Coast
Solution

IN 1990, THE DENVER BRONCOS COULD LOOK BACK IN triumph at a decade that had seen them play in three Super Bowls and maintain their grip on Colorado's cutting edge.

An ongoing competition with the faltering Denver Nuggets for the hearts and minds of Rocky Mountain sports fans was no contest.

But six years later, the charming, fan-friendly Colorado Rockies owned a huge chunk of the market, the Colorado Avalanche owned the Stanley Cup, Coors Field was the hip place to be, and the Nuggets and Avalanche were proceeding on a plan to build a state-of-the-art arena to increase revenue flow and the flow of fans who increasingly flock to the NBA and NHL.

Meanwhile, the Broncos hadn't made the playoffs in two seasons, hadn't hosted a playoff game since 1991, had a virtual .500 record for the decade, and were playing catch-up in the city they'd once owned.

Owner Pat Bowlen was growing desperate.

He said he needed a taxpayer-supported new stadium to survive in the 21st century. But his lobbyists had to go into overtime at the General Assembly just to pass a bill that would place a proposal for a new stadium on the ballot. It made it by one vote. Polls showed it'd be even harder to persuade tax-payers to approve it, in part because of Bowlen himself; or at least the image of him, which crystallized when he was photographed walking the Mile High Stadium sideline wearing an ankle-length raccoon-fur coat, like a gilded character from Dynasty,

The Broncos won **12** of their first **13** games in **1996**, thanks in large part to Shanahan's high-scoring offense, which overwhelmed many opponents. The Broncos finished first in the league in total offense thanks in large part to the addition of running back Terrell Davis (#30).

detractors said.

John Elway was growing desperate, as well. His career clock was ticking down, persistently, and he was worn with toil from carrying the franchise on his back since 1983. Since Bowlen's chances for a new stadium were tied directly to the team's success, the moment was fraught with the future for Elway, as well.

Enter Mike Shanahan.

"I kept thinking, 'Mike is really the guy I want in here,' " Bowlen said about the Phillips' years.

Bowlen and Elway needed a Super Bowl title. It was up to Shanahan to take care of the details, of which he is a dexterous master.

When Mike Heimerdinger was a graduate assistant at Florida, Shanahan, then the school's offensive coordinator, asked him to diagram some defensive alignments. Heimerdinger did it, but Shanahan, dedicated to little things and big, handed it back. The line of scrimmage was slightly crooked.

"Do it again," Shanahan said.

Heimerdinger completed another diagram, gave it to Shanahan, who handed it back once more. The squares were not symmetrical.

"Do it again," Shanahan said.

Heimerdinger, now a Broncos assistant coach, got it right the third time.

Shanahan never shuts down, even during his down time. Every year his family and five other clans gather in Palm Springs for a vacation. Shanahan makes all the plane reservations, arranges for hotel rooms, sets up tee times, takes care of dinner reservations and coordinates the arrivals and departures of each family's plane. Then he types the information on a "minute-by-minute" itinerary which he then sends to each family.

A control freak? To the max.

Shanahan's athletic career ended when he suffered a serious injury his junior season in college, which cost him a kidney. But that only re-doubled his passion to

Elway calls Terrell Davis the best back he's played with in Denver. In 1995, Davis finished with 176 yards on 20 carries against San Diego. He carried the ball six consecutive times on the final game-winning drive, setting up a last-second Jason Elam field goal.

make his mark. During his first NFL job, he transformed Elway into a Pro Bowler, then became the Los Angeles Raiders head coach in 1988. That ended when Al Davis fired him in the midst of the 1989 season.

"You can't have Colin Powell and Norman Schwartzkopf on the same battle-field," Broncos tight end Shannon Sharpe said. "Either one or the other. One had to be in D.C., one had to be overseas."

Shanahan returned to the Broncos in time to help them advance to the 1989 Super Bowl, was fired by Dan Reeves after the 1991 season, and then left to become offensive coordinator of the San Francisco 49ers, where he took a stratospheric offense to even rarer heights.

In every way, Shanahan had been preparing all his life for the opportunity of his life, which Bowlen gave him in the form of a seven-year contract with complete authority over all football operations.

"Thank God he wanted complete control," Bowlen said.

During four spring and summer mini-camps, Shanahan laid the foundation for his offense and defense, established a sense of camaraderie and implemented a spartan work regimen that left no room for complacency. It was no picnic, as a radio talk show host discovered when he entered the practice area with some munchies during the second mini-camp. He was soon without his lunch.

"I can tell we've worked hard every time I get out of bed. It's like the '80s again," defensive end Simon Fletcher said.

"Back in the '80s, it was an old team and everyone had a chance to jell," wide receiver Vance Johnson said. "Teams have to have a chance to jell. It's important to get that camaraderie started. That's the reason for all the camps."

Saccomano remained a true believer. After an afternoon practice in May, as he was driving home, his car was virtually totaled after a driver blew a red light at 55 mph. Saccomano emerged without serious injury, and even managed to have a heart-to-heart with the investigating officer.

"The cop was saying, 'I'm the biggest Bronco fan there is. I've got $3,000 of Bronco memorabilia in my house,'" Saccomano said. "Then he said, 'You don't even have to tell me the Broncos are going to be back. I know it's going to be a big year.'

"The cop feels it. I feel it. Everyone feels it. Mike is back, and everything is back to normal."

Not quite. The championship season was another year away. In 1995, the Broncos finished with an 8-8 record, which satisfied no one. During training camp, Elway struggled to get a confident grip on Shanahan's West Coast scheme, a more sophisticated and finely tuned version of Fassel's.

"It's the hardest camp since my first couple years," Elway said. "It's not too bad physically, because I'm in pretty good shape. It's been more mental than anything.

"I've had to concentrate a lot harder. It's been a real challenge because I'm starting all over. It's from wanting to be perfect. When I lose that, I quit. I'd be worried if I didn't get frustrated. It comes from expectations, too. I expect a lot more from my 13th year than my first."

The Broncos beat Buffalo 22-7 in the season-opener at Mile High, a particularly painful defeat for Wade Phillips, now the Bills' defensive coordinator. They lost to Dallas 31-21 the next week in Dallas, then returned to Mile High Stadium to face the Washington Redskins.

On the game's final play, Elway stepped back to midfield, dodged the rush, then heaved a perfect bomb to Rod Smith, whose leaping catch lifted Denver to a 38-31 victory.

"To tell you the truth, I've never really had one where we scored a touchdown on the last play of the game," Elway said.

"That has to be the biggest play I've seen since I've been playing pro sports, and I've seen a lot," safety Steve Atwater said.

But during a 17-6 loss to San Diego seven days later, the Broncos failed to score a touchdown for the first time since Nov. 22, 1992, when Tommy Maddox replaced Elway in a 24-0 shutout loss to the Raiders. The last time Elway had gone without a touchdown was Oct. 12, 1992, when Washington won 34-3.

"I'm shocked," receiver Mike Pritchard said.

Elway had a rare day off in 1996 when the Broncos met Green Bay, the eventual Super Bowl Champions, in Game 15. He had a sore left hamstring. It was the first start he'd missed since Dec. 22, 1994 (left knee strain) and only the 10th in 14 seasons because of injury.

The following week in Seattle, the Broncos managed to score a touchdown, but just one, a 26-yard pass from Elway to Pritchard. The Seahawks won 27-10, and Denver had a 2-3 record, only one game ahead of Phillips' record at that point the year before.

"Everyone looks forward to playing the Denver Broncos right now," defensive tackle Michael Dean Perry said. "If I was a team getting ready to play us, I'd be licking my chops."

Added Elway: "We're looking for answers everywhere."

The answer turned out to be the shotgun. In the first dramatic departure from his West Coast scheme, Shanahan put Elway back in his comfort zone, and he responded by completing 21 of 34 passes for 287 yards, and two touchdowns during a 37-3 win over New England. It was the second-widest margin of victory on the road in club history.

"This is an awesome feeling," Elway said. "We just knocked 'em out."

Elway, however, got KO'd the following week in Philadelphia. On the first play of the second quarter, he went down — then to the sideline — after a blow to the head that induced a concussion. Elway couldn't come back, and neither could the Broncos, who suffered a 31-13 defeat.

"Coming into the season John had such high expectations," Sharpe said. "We had this new offense. We had Mike Shanahan. Everything seemed perfect. And here we are pretty much in the same position as we were last year. He's getting kind of frustrated saying, 'What do we have to do? What do I have to do to get to the next level?' We blew some opportunities to make the playoffs this year, and that really bummed him out."

As the frustrating, erratic season progressed, the most significant development became the rise of Terrell Davis. The soft-spoken rookie from Georgia was the 196th player and 21st back selected in the 1995 draft, but he was Denver's starter by late August. He ran for 97 yards and scored his fourth touchdown against New England; rushed for 135 yards on 22 carries four weeks later against Arizona; and became the lowest-drafted rookie ever to run for 1,000 yards against Jacksonville in Game 13.

"He's the best running back I've ever played with in Denver," Elway said. "He can do it all, and well."

Davis' greatest asset, in fact, is that he has several. He can run with power up the middle, swing the ball outside, block with power and catch the ball like a skilled receiver, which merits more than passing praise from Shanahan.

But Davis entered a new realm on November 19 against San Diego, finishing with 176 yards on 30 carries — the third-best rushing performance in club history. Nevertheless, the score was tied 27-27 with 3:34 left. It was time for Elway to go into comeback mode, as the scoreboard graphic made pointedly clear: "John Elway, most game-saving drives (35) in NFL history."

But this time, Elway went along for the ride.

On the first play of the Broncos' final drive, he handed off to Davis, then watched, motionless as a statue, as the rookie ran through the heart of the Chargers' defense. On the second play, Elway gave the ball to Davis once again. On the third, he handed it right back to him. In all, Davis carried the ball six consecutive times, gaining 53 of his 176 yards as the Broncos positioned themselves for Jason Elam's 32-yard, game-winning field goal with two seconds remaining.

Davis had carried Denver to victory, and into a new era. Elway finally had a running alternative to his long-running solo act.

The times were changing in Denver, but not the Broncos' fortunes. The offense ranked No. 1 in the AFC, but the defense, though improved, remained erratic.

The Broncos' playoff hopes ended in Week 15 with a 20-17 loss to Kansas City at Arrowhead Stadium. A funeral gloom descended on the team when cornerback Lionel Washington was knocked unconscious after colliding with teammate Steve Atwater. After lying motionless for 10 minutes, he was put on a stretcher and rushed to the hospital, where doctors later determined he'd suffered a concussion, but no paralysis, as many had feared.

The Broncos tried to salvage a disastrous day, but no one needed to tell Elway that this wouldn't be the scene of one of his miracle comebacks.

In a weary monotone afterward, he talked openly about retirement. Later he said he wanted to discuss his future with Janet and his father before reaching a decision.

"I'm definitely going to listen to what they have to say," he said. "But I think the bottom line is I've got to make the decision, what's right and wrong. But I want to get their feedback and see what they think. I don't want to rush into anything. Everyone's talking about what I want to do. I think the Broncos have to figure out what they want to do."

Elway wondered aloud if the Broncos even wanted him back, prompting a quick reply from Shanahan.

"Once his athletic ability starts going in a different direction, then it'll be my time to step in and say: 'Hey John, this is what I think.' he said. "But I don't see that. He's made some throws this year that I didn't think he could make. So I think he's got a number of years ahead of him if he wants to pay the price in the off-season."

Actually, the franchise needed Elway more than ever. Denver had changed since Elway's arrival, and no one knew that better than Bowlen, who finally convinced his franchise player to sign a new five-year deal in the spring of '96.

Colorado had caught a major-league case of baseball fever (on its own).

In 1993, 5,000 people showed up to watch the Rockies' first workout. After its first 21 home games, Colorado had topped the Cleveland Indians' entire 1992 attendance. In their first two months, the Rockies broke four major league attendance records: largest-ever Opening Day Crowd (80,227), largest crowd for a three-game series (212,475), a four-game series (251,447) and fewest games needed to draw a million (17).

That was only the start. The Rockies' phenomenon caught everyone off guard — the Rockies included. By the time Coors Field opened, the franchise not only possessed baseball's most passionate and numerous fans, but a sun-kissed, nostalgia-blissed state-of-the-art facility that was the envy of the baseball world — and Bowlen.

"Denver has grown from a relatively small Midwestern city to a much more sophisticated city than it even was when I came in 1984," Bowlen said. "They've been through a recession, they've recovered, there are all kinds of people moving into the state, not just into Denver. So what you're really seeing is a much more sophisticated sports fan than you had 10, 12, 15 years ago."

Before the game against the Packers, Elway exchanged words with quarterback Brett Favre, whose game has been compared to Elway's. Favre went on to win the Super Bowl, and Elway was left to wait for another season.

Elway's career was revived in **1995** with the arrival of head coach Mike Shanahan who had earlier been his quarterback guru in Denver.

Elway waves to the Mile High crowd.

Denver fans were cool to Elway following his shaky start, but over the years he's become a Rocky Mountain institution, as well as an ambassador for Colorado. There are stories he might run for political office when his playing days are over.

Over the years Elway has taken a pounding, especially in 1994 when he was sacked 46 times. One of the worst beatings came during a 42-19 loss to San Francisco in week 15, which forced him to the sideline prematurely.

Many of John Elway's greatest – and roughest – moments have come against the Kansas City Chiefs (seen here being sacked by Derrick Thomas #58).

Elway has competed against many quarterbacks, but few as resilient as Dave Krieg.

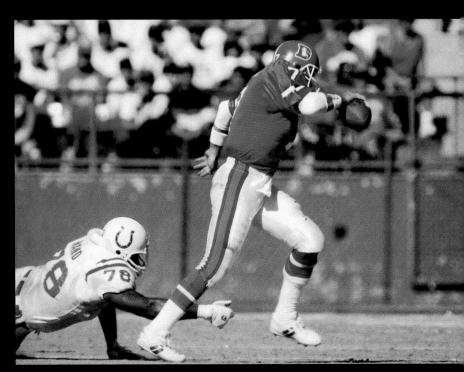

Defenders insist Elway has a "sixth-sense" that allows him to escape the grasp of a tackler at the last frustrating moment.

The Broncos and 49ers lead the league in international travel. Both are regular participants in overseas pre-season games. Jerry Rice, Steve Young, Anthony Miller and Elway pose here in Japan.

Jack Elway always taught his son to be ready to use his legs as well as his arms and wits. Even in the twilight of his career, Elway is considered one of the league's best running quarterbacks.

Elway's arrival in Denver was prime-time news. More than 50 media members gathered in Greeley for his first training camp. Here he's shown posing for a cover story.

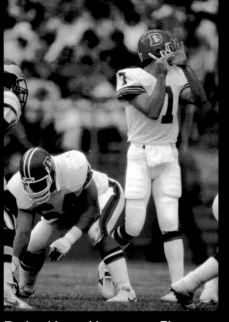

During his rookie season. Elway was often bewildered by the complexities of the pro game. For example, he lined up behind his guard, rather than center.

By 1986, Elway had grown comfortable in his role as the Broncos quarterback and leader. Around his teammates, he insisted on being "one of the guys".

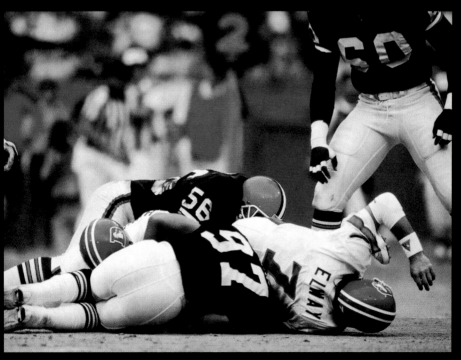

Although an expert at dodging trouble, even No. 7 can't stay on his feet

The original Broncos fans were now part of the graying generation that had a lockhold at Mile High Stadium, where the average season ticket-holder is fifty-something.

Their sons and daughters and the latest wave of newcomers were obsessed with the Rockies, Avalanche — and maybe the Broncos.

To Generation X — and now Y — and the advertisers who covet their young and extreme purchasing power, the Broncos and their mummified memories belonged to yesterday's cutting edge.

"Many from an entire generation have never seen a Bronco game," said Rosemary Hanratty, the Broncos' ex-marketing director. "How do you combat that fact? That's the Broncos' real challenge in the next few years. It's hard to compete with the new. It's very hard to compete with the new and winning, like the Rockies and Avalanche."

In focus group research in the Denver area, twenty-somethings were shown pictures of Avalanche and Broncos players and asked to link them with a car. For the Avalanche they chose a Viper ("cool and hip")' for the Broncos a Cadillac. ("old and traditional").

"We're definitely not chic these days," Saccomano said.

Carl Scheer, former president of the Nuggets, said the Broncos had imperiled their future by not actively recruiting replacements for veteran fans.

"I always felt there was an arrogance about the Broncos. They just sent out tickets once a year and put the marketing staff to sleep," he said. "For so long, they could afford to throw out the proverbial football and expect to be adored. And they were. Not now.

"The aging process has really affected their fans. They've become middle-aged as far as consumer types. The (20-45) crowd is where it's all at in the minds of advertisers. The young hip crowd makes things happen. And people want to be where it's all happening."

In the Gray '90s, the Broncos' sense of eminent domain had been eroded as well by Lodo, a rejuvenated area surrounding Coors Field, where the Broncos' Lost Generation routinely congregates, often before and after Rockies' games.

The Broncos were also concerned with the following generation. In fact, with youngsters choosing to play soccer rather than football, coupled with all the team's new competition, the Broncos were on the verge of losing two generations.

"The future of professional sports is not just with the product on the field — it's how you present it," Scheer said. "In the last half of this decade and in the 21st century, consumers are going to demand the amenities of modern facilities. Mile High doesn't cut it any more."

The Broncos had to get a new stadium, but they needed to win a Super Bowl to guarantee one.

They got off to a fast start in '96, beating the New York Jets 31-6 in a season-opener at Mile High Stadium. The defense, bolstered by the addition of defensive end Alfred Williams, a free-agent acquisition from the 49ers, and linebacker Bill Romanowski, a free agent from the Philadelphia Eagles, piled up nine sacks, forcing quarterback Neil O'Donnell to run for his life in his Jets debut.

The following week the Broncos beat Seattle 30-20 in the Kingdome. Nevertheless, Elway struggled to find his rhythm, prompting a new round of questions about his age and its effect on his game. The Broncos were ranked No. 1 in the NFL in rushing, and Sharpe, Anthony Miller and McCaffrey were little more than diversionary props.

Elway hoped for a breakthrough two weeks later in Kansas City. Instead, he ended Denver's hopes when he threw into double coverage late in the game, and into the hands of Kansas City cornerback Dale Carter, rather than to Sharpe, who was wide open deep in Chiefs' territory. For the third time, Elway had failed to pass for 200 yards, and for the first time in 15 games, he had failed to throw a touchdown pass. In four games, he'd averaged 183 yards passing and thrown six interceptions compared with five touchdowns.

"I'm not playing up to the expectations I have of myself," he said after the 17-14 loss.

In fact, Elway compared himself to a lawn ornament.

"I was kind of feeling like an iron deer in my front yard," he said. "I had to start playing my game again. I wasn't moving around there or making plays."

Elway's running commentary paid off the following week during a 14-10 win over Cincinnati. Stepping back into the shotgun, he completed 23 of 37 passes for 335 yards, and two touchdowns, including a perfect pump-and-throw to Anthony Miller for what proved to be the game-winning 23-yard touchdown.

The following week he completed 32 of 41 passes for 323 yards and four touchdowns during a 28-17 win over San Diego, and the week after that he was 25 of 39 for 326 yards and three touchdowns during a 45-34 victory over the Baltimore Ravens.

"During the past three weeks I don't know that anyone has played any better," Kansas City coach Marty Schottenheimer said.

After seven games Elway had thrown for 1,712 yards and 14 touchdowns, completed 63.2 percent of his passes, was on track to set personal records in touchdowns and completion percentage, and was close to the pace he needed for his second 4,000-yard season.

"We've taken a lot of pressure off John," Sharpe said. "We don't ask him to throw the ball 50 times a game. We don't ask him to throw the ball 60 yards down the field. We ask him to just not make mistakes and put the ball in the guys' hands and let guys make plays for him. So far, we've been able to do that. For so long, he had to carry the team. He was all the offense we had."

During a 34-7 win over Kansas City on Oct. 27, Elway ran for a career-high 62 yards and passed for 286 yards and three touchdowns, and in the process became only the second quarterback in NFL history to reach 40,000 yards passing and 3,000 yards rushing.

During a Monday night showdown on November 4 in Oakland, Elway ran for a career-best yardage (70) for the second week in a row. He also went into comeback mode. With seven minutes left, and Oakland leading 21-16 on its home field, he completed several short passes to move to the Raiders' 49. On third and 10, he pump-faked a rainbow scoring bomb to Rod Smith, who had badly beaten Raiders cornerback Larry Brown.

"It was the scariest throw of my life because Rod was so wide open," Elway said following the 22-21 win, which improved Denver's record to 8-1.

The Bronco's clinched the AFC West title and home-field advantage through the playoffs on Dec. 1, then had to play their final three regular-season games with nothing on the line. The Broncos lost two of those three, including the regular-season finale against San Diego. After that game, Shanahan addressed the team.

Pat Bowlen found Mike Shanahan in the locker room. "We didn't have to say anything," Bowlen said after he embraced his head coach. "He knows what it means to me to beat the Raiders, and I know what it means to beat the Raiders."

Rocky Mountain News columnist Bob Kravitz wrote: "Now we can say it: This is the best team in the AFC. Period. Exclamation point. Another exclamation point. Period."

The Broncos continued their joyride in ensuing weeks, thanks to a touch of serendipity.

In Week 10, the Chicago Bears had the ball, first down, on Denver's 1, trailing 17-12 with 40 seconds remaining. Bill Romanowski's heart was kicking against his ribs. Alfred Williams was running on desperation. And they were the calm ones.

On first down, Raymont Harris, averaging five yards per carry, was stuffed by Williams for a 1-yard loss. On second down, the Bears sent Harris around left end, only to have Romanowski dump him for a 2-yard loss.

On third down, Jim Flanigan, a defensive tackle lined up as an eligible receiver, stepped into the end zone, unnoticed by preoccupied defenders. Dave Krieg floated a pass that any prep player would have caught without second thought, but Flanigan dropped it, shocking the Broncos even more than himself.

On fourth down, Denver safety Tyrone Braxton knocked away Krieg's final pass in the right corner of the end zone. The Broncos had an NFL-best 9-1 record, plus a two-game lead over their nearest AFC challenger.

"We have lady luck on our side," Michael Dean Perry said.

Two weeks later, Elway completed 27 of 36 passes for 334 yards and two touchdowns against Minnesota, and, his most dramatic comeback win of the season. With 19 seconds left, on third down, he fired to Sharpe in the end zone. Vikings safety Harlon Barnett tipped it once, then twice; teammate Orlando Thomas tipped it a third time, and into the hands of Broncos receiver Ed McCaffrey, who tumbled into the end zone. The Broncos were winners.

"This white jersey came out of nowhere. It was Eddie McCaffrey, and he had it in the end zone," Elway said after the victory.

By that point, Elway had completed 245 of his 397 passes (61.7 percent) for 2,887 yards and 23 touchdowns — for a 89.5 quarterback rating.

Since Game Four, he'd completed 172 of 282 passes (61 percent) for 2,195 yards and 18 touchdowns, and compiled a 95.8 quarterback rating.

"This is the best team I've been on, we're winning, and I'm throwing the ball as well as I've ever thrown it," he said. "I don't think my arm is as strong as it was back then. But I'm more accurate now. I'm throwing it in easier spots for them to catch it. I've never felt more comfortable and confident going into games. I've never had more confidence in people around me — players and coaches.

"After four years of being a kind of mediocre team, it's definitely a big, big bonus to be winning this late in a career."

On the following Sunday, the Broncos beat Seattle 34-7 at Mile High Stadium to clinch the AFC West title. Much to the Broncos' surprise, Pittsburgh and Buffalo lost that day. So on a single Sunday, the Broncos secured what many thought would take a month of Sundays: home-field advantage throughout the playoffs.

It was a horrible break. Denver's next meaningful game was five weeks away.

"You don't want to go into the playoffs that way," said expert analysts across the country. "The teams that are hot at the end of the season have the advantage in the playoffs. This is not a good thing for Denver."

The following week, Elway remained on the sideline with a sore hamstring while the Broncos suffered a 41-6 loss in Green Bay. The next Sunday he completed 19 of 31 passes for 206 yards and one touchdown during a 24-19 win over Oakland. Elway played sparingly during the final Sunday of the regular season as the Broncos lost once more, to San Diego.

When the Jacksonville Jaguars beat Buffalo in the first round of the AFC Divisional playoffs, they earned a trip to Denver to play the Broncos. NBC-TV began making preparations for this second-round game at Mile High Stadium

— and the AFC Championship game the following week. Few figured Jacksonville would beat Denver, or could.

"They've got enough talent to beat anybody," warned Elway, who hadn't appeared in a playoff game since 1993 and one at Mile High Stadium since 1991. "They have enough talent to come in and beat us. Hopefully, we can keep everything under control and play our football."

None of the NFL's previous eight expansion teams had won more than three games in their first season, and their combined overall record for the first six seasons was 17-92-11. Dallas went 0-11-1 in 1960, its debut season. Tampa Bay lost 26 consecutive games before victory No. 1. Following another numbing loss, Buccaneers coach John McKay was too weary for speeches. Instead, he said, "if anyone needs a shower, take one."

A reporter asked McKay, "How do you feel about your team's execution?"

"Personally," he replied. "I'm all for it. Go ahead."

On September 17, 1967, rookie John Gilliam bowed his head in prayer on the opening kickoff of New Orleans' opening game.

"I was praying, 'Please don't let the ball come to me,'" he recalled.

It did, and seven seconds later Gilliam found himself in the end zone on the stirring end of a 94-yard touchdown run, imbibing in the atmosphere caused by 80,000 enchanted fans at Tulane Stadium. The Saints ended the season in last place, and before long fans began putting paper sacks over their heads to protest the team's awful play.

Thanks to free agency, however, Jacksonville and Carolina were free to pursue any player who might also have been lured by established teams. They also were given extra draft picks, which is why both advanced to post-season play in Year Two. Nevertheless, Jacksonville quarterback Mark Brunell received a first-class reality check when NBC-TV analyst Cris Collingsworth asked a question that presumed the fourth-year quarterback is right-handed. Brunell is left-handed.

"That was interesting," Brunell said. "You would think that Collingsworth would know that."

Brunell had a way to go before he closed the celebrity gap with Steve Young,

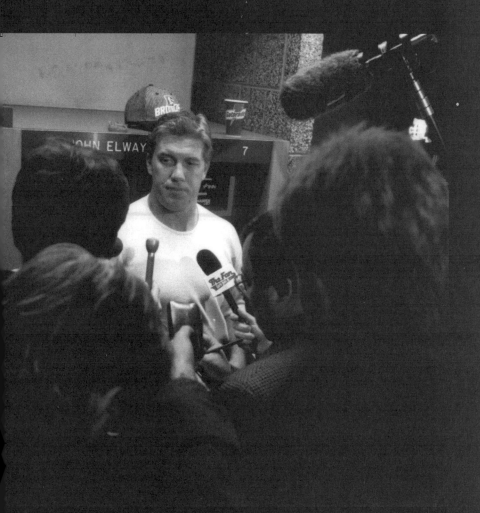

Against all odds, the Broncos lost an AFC Divisional playoff game to Jacksonville, at Mile High Stadium. It was one of the biggest upsets in recent NFL playoff history. Elway - shown here addressing the press - said the defeat hurt more than the Super Bowl losses.

with whom he often is compared because of his speed, mobility and left-handed darts. Still, he became the first quarterback since Johnny Unitas in 1963 to lead all quarterbacks in rushing (396 yards) and passing (4,367).

"Rushing is something I've been blessed with," he said. "If you have it, use it."

The Broncos jumped to a 12-0 lead on Elway's arm and legs.

Then, almost strangely, the offense ground to a halt, and Denver abandoned its running game, with the score still close. Elway jumped-started his team later in the no-huddle, but it was too late to avert defeat. In addition, the Broncos' special teams were anything but.

But it was Denver's defense, which had risen from the ashes in '96, that crumbled when it mattered most. Natrone Means ran over and through the Broncos, finishing with 140 yards and 6.7 yards per carry. Brunell completed 18 of 29 passes for 245 yards, ran for 44 more, and transformed the Broncos into a bunch of Keystone Cops with madcap scrambles.

It all caught up with Bill Romanowski — all the futile chasing and running around for nothing except the chance to stop an embarrassing spectacle the next time.

"It's devastating to play as hard and well as we did all year long and then come up short," he said.

Michael Dean Perry ran out of answers and energy, as well. Late in the third quarter, the Broncos finally got a break when Willie Jackson stepped out of bounds while catching a Brunell third-down pass. The Jaguars' and Broncos' special teams trotted onto the field, as Perry walked slowly to the Broncos' sideline at Mile High Stadium. Too slowly, it turned out, because the Broncos were penalized for having too many men on the field, none of whom ever consistently stopped Brunell during Jacksonville's 30-27 upset victory.

Instead of fourth and five, the Jaguars had a first down, and a few minutes later, a field goal. After watching Jacksonville score on its final six possessions, Pat Bowlen compared the defeat to a disastrous 24-17 playoff loss to Pittsburgh in 1984.

The Broncos three main men - Elway, Shanahan and Bowlen - hope to lead the club into the next century, as well as a Super Bowl title. They also hope to convince local voters to approve the financing of a new stadium.

"I've said all year this is the best team I've ever been associated with. I still believe that. We just had a meltdown at a time we didn't have to," Bowlen said. "We won't forget this for a long, long time."

Added Perry: "Unbelievable. We had it all in front of us. Home field, everything. And then for the defense to play its worst game of the year … it's just unbelievable."

Elway, who completed 287 of 466 pass attempts (61.8 percent) for 3,282 yards and 26 touchdowns, and rushed for 249 yards and four TDs during his 14th season, dropped from sight afterward.

"I haven't committed hara-kiri yet, but I've thought about it for a month. I'm not sure I'll ever get over it. That's as disappointed as I've ever been. You can talk about the Super Bowl losses or anything. There's not one that comes close to this," Elway said.

Elway ranks among the most resilient quarterbacks in NFL history. He's played on despite bruised biceps, thighs, and buttocks, a fractured rib, sprained fingers, knees, elbows...

Chapter 10 —
The Home Stretch

IN 1986, JOHN ELWAY LOOKED ACROSS THE LOCKER ROOM AT an ancient, bandaged teammate, who'd played 14 seasons for the Denver Broncos. Then he tried to picture himself in his 14th season in Denver.

That was a pocket of thought Elway couldn't enter back then. Or even find. "It was mind-boggling to even think about," Elway said.

It's reality now.

In early September of the 1996 season, in Seattle, Elway played in his 192nd game for the Broncos, breaking the franchise record set by Tom Jackson, a linebacker, from 1973-86. After his first season in Denver, Elway didn't know what to expect from Year Two. Now he and the Broncos are tethered for the ages in football lore. In an era of itinerant players and fleeting partnerships, Elway-Denver is like Layne-Detroit, Unitas-Baltimore, Staubach-Dallas, Bradshaw-Pittsburgh.

Elway is also tethered in quarterback lore with Layne, Unitas, Staubach, Bradshaw, Montana and Marino. He might not be the best quarterback ever. On the other hand, his best days aren't over, either.

While peers deal with brittle bones and passing effectiveness, Elway is still armed for mass production. In fact, three of his best four NFL seasons occurred from 1993-96. His 1983 classmates aren't faring as well.

Jim Kelly retired after the '96 season, and Marino, hobbled by injuries, looks and feels ancient. Only Elway has transformed the autumn of his career into his golden years.

"This is the most confidence I've had," he said. "It's a combination of different things. It's a combination of the system, my experience, the people we have

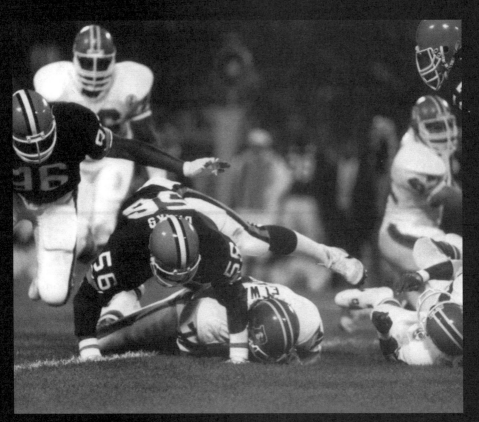

Every NFL defender wants to get a piece of Elway, who has fallen many times only to get back on his feet and win again. "You've got to be a little lucky, but there's no question the weight work has helped my durability and endurance at the end of games."

running it and the people around me. It's fun to be in my position."

Added Mike Shanahan: "I don't see how a quarterback can be playing any better."

Elias Sports Bureau stats chief Steve Hirdt told *Sports Illustrated* that if Elway stays healthy and with Shanahan, "he could conceivably own every major passing record there is before he's through."

The irony is unsurpassed for Elway.

For a decade, he labored in a system that restrained his ultimate talents until that system broke down and left him to his own improvisational devices. Meanwhile Marino and Montana put up stratospheric numbers by merely operating their offenses routinely.

Now Elway is using a user-friendly system to record-breaking advantage. In Wade Phillips' first year, Elway threw for 4,030 yards and finished with a 92.8 quarterback rating, both team records. In 1994, despite missing two games, he passed for 3,490 yards and 16 TDS and had a 85.7 QB rating. In 1995 he finished with 3,970 yards, 26 TDS and an 86.3 rating. In '96, Elway's numbers declined as soon as the Broncos clinched the AFC West title and home-field advantage for the playoffs. Elway was more concerned with preparing for the playoffs.

Nevertheless, he still finished with 3,328 yards, led all AFC quarterbacks with a 89.2 rating, and ranked second in completion percentage (61.6) and third in TD passes (26).

He also became the winningest quarterback in NFL history (126 wins), finished second in Associated Press NFL Most Valuable Player balloting, was named the AFC Offensive Player of the Month for October, set a new NFL record for career rushing attempts by a quarterback (687), and rose to third all-time in the NFL in pass attempts (6,392 yards), passing yards (45,034) and total yards (48,129).

Yet numbers aren't the heart of Elway's game. They never were. At the heart of Elway's game is his, well, heart.

While Joe Montana and Dan Marino had all-star casts, Elway had to struggle to

Quarterbacks are increasingly at risk in the NFL, despite steps taken to better protect them. "I'm not sure you can even protect pocket passers any more," Green Bay Offense Coordinator Sherman Lewis said.

survive, much less thrive, for a decade.

Over the years, he's used 57 wide receivers, and the three most prominent ones — Mark Jackson, Vance Johnson and Ricky Nattiel — will never enter the Hall of Fame unless they pay the regular admission price. Until Terrell Davis, Elway's running backs were secondary concerns for defenses.

Entering the 1993 season, Elway had been protected by only one Pro Bowl offensive lineman — Keith Bishop.

Elway has also played on despite innumerable injuries, including bruised biceps, thighs and buttocks, a fractured rib, turf burn, turf toe, pulled hamstrings, groin pulls, swollen elbow, swollen knees, elbow sprains, finger sprains, knee sprains, splitting headaches ...

In the same time span, other NFL teams have run through 212 starting quarterbacks, including 110 in the NFC and 102 in the AFC.

Some went out on stretchers. In fact, in the '90s, QBS are an endangered species. The headhunters are loose, and heads are falling, making Elway's long run even more telling.

In 1993, as he headed to the sideline at Texas Stadium, Dallas quarterback Troy Aikman appeared coherent. A knee to the side of his head had left him faintly wobbly in the NFC Championship game against San Francisco.

But no one suspected trouble until Aikman reached the sideline.

Center Mark Stepnoski, who had been on crutches for several weeks following knee surgery, was the first to greet the Pro Bowl quarterback. Aikman was shocked to see Stepnoski on crutches.

"What happened to you?" he asked.

Stepnoski quickly summoned the team trainer, who asked Aikman a series of questions to determine the extent of his head injury, including "Where will (the Super Bowl) be played?"

"Henryetta" Aikman said.

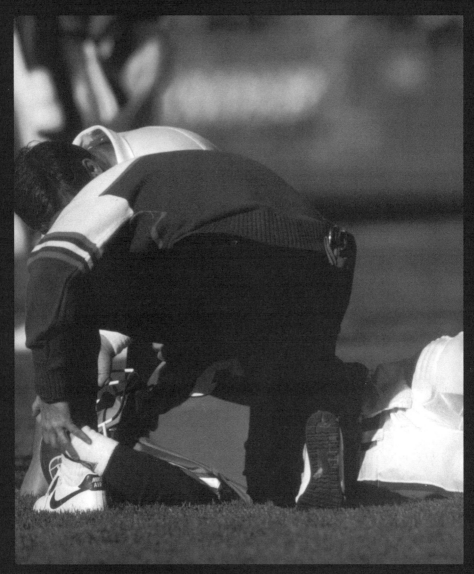

Elway had been sacked **462** times for **3,442** yards by **1997**, more than any other active player since Dave Krieg and fourth most of all quarterbacks since **1963**.

Henryetta, Oklahoma, is Aikman's home town, which is about as far removed from Atlanta — the site of that season's Super Bowl — as Aikman was from reality. Strike another blow for the menacing power of concussions, which have become a disturbingly frequent — and perhaps unconscionable — staple of NFL life. In 1995, an average of four players per weekend went down with concussions, including Elway, who got back on his feet and started the following week.

The images are haunting: Buffalo receiver Don Beebe, on his back, out cold, with one forearm pointing stiffly in the air; the Rams' Chris Miller sitting upright on the field following a savage hit, except for his head, which is dangling face down.

Part of the problem stems from physics. Players are bigger and faster, and mass plus speed equals devastating collisions. But there's another element at work, as well, says former Giants quarterback Phil Simms.

"Years before, everyone was a little more careful," he said. "They didn't want to make a big mistake. Now players are definitely on the edge more. They're willing to take more chances to get the big hit, to intercept passes, to make the catch. They're willing to face disaster."

Violence has always been part of NFL lore. According to former Colts' defensive lineman Art Donovan, the NFL of the '50s was populated by "oversized coal miners and West Texas psychopaths."

Hardy Brown, who played for seven teams in his bone-crushing, 10-year pro career, was one of that era's most menacing players. His right shoulder was his primary weapon. He usually aimed at opponents' heads, resulting in broken necks, cheeks, jaws and innumerable concussions.

In 1953, Eagles running back Toy Ledbetter was heading around the right end against the 49ers, then Brown's employer. "I usually kept my eye on (Brown), but this time I cut inside a block and I never saw him," Ledbetter said years later. "He caught me with a shoulder, and the next thing I knew I was on the ground looking for my head."

A team doctor said Ledbetter had suffered the worst facial fracture he'd ever seen.

Concussions have become a disturbingly routine part of the NFL in the 90's. In 1995, an average of four players per weekend went down with them, including Elway during a prime-time game against Philadelphia.

Could it ever get that brutal again? Former Oakland Raiders defensive end Howie Long wonders.

"Hunting season is on. It's not a pretty picture for quarterbacks," Long said.

Yet Elway continues to dodge disaster, because he can.

He can veer and cut and run while buying time to pass. Or he can convert himself into a halfback and head downfield in a tearing hurry. In fact, Elway runs an offense '90s style — on the run.

"I'm not sure you can even protect pocket passers anymore, even with a really talented offensive line," Green Bay offensive coordinator Sherman Lewis said. "Defensive linemen are just too big and too fast these days. You gotta be able to move and throw on the run. And when you do that, you make life extremely hard on the defense."

Elway's durability also stems from his demanding conditioning and weight-training regimens.

He missed one game in 1984 with a shoulder injury, a 1988 game with a sprained right ankle and one in '89 because of the flu. Elway knew he couldn't remain that durable forever, so his revolt against fate reached a new extreme in 1994, when he began a year-round, full-body weight program. He added a full-scale running program two years later.

On a typical summer day he was sucking wind while pulling a 200-pound iron sled across an empty practice field. Or gasping for air on a step-mill as his pulse rate soared to 180 and his mind drifted into bleak reveries. Or pumping iron in the team's weight room, his home sweet hell.

One day teammate Rod Smith decided to call it a day before he'd completed his routine. "I've been doing this for 13 years, and you're tired!" Elway called to the third-year wide receiver.

"I can't allow myself to get out of shape because at my age it's so hard to get back in shape, so I started doing it year-round," Elway said. "I don't do it for bulk. I don't do it for strength. I do it for durability.

"You've got to be a little lucky, but there's no question the weight work has really helped my durability and my endurance at the end of games."

The games remain a dose of oxygen to Elway.

Even now, after all the years and wounds, they have the grace of a dream to a man who still smiles when he recalls the days in Missoula, when he and his dad would play one-on-one in the backyard, John yelling "one more, one more, one more," at the end.

On December 1, 1996, the Broncos beat Seattle 34-7 to clinch the AFC West title and home-field advantage through the playoffs. After he'd met with the press, showered, chatted with teammates and lingered for a while, Elway returned to the field, where his parents and family awaited in the gathering dark.

But after spotting a dozen kids playing football on the churned-up Mile High turf, he trotted over to join them, pulled hamstring and all. Then John Elway — still a dream-chasing teenager at heart — began playing catch with a bunch of kids on the same field on which he has established himself as one of the greatest quarterbacks ever to play the game of football.

Some of those kids probably hadn't been born in 1983, when John's father, in a reflective mood, watched his son leave for the NFL, and a place in history, a job of a lifetime essentially completed.

"I'd feel real successful if I could just preserve for John the joy of playing ball. Because that's where he'll find his greatness," Jack Elway said at the time.

Super Bowl ring or not - he already has.

Photography Credits